Tempted No More

Breaking Free of Pornography By Walking in Grace

Eddie Snipes

A book by:
Exchanged Life Discipleship

Copyright © 2015 by Eddie Snipes and
Exchanged Life Discipleship

http://www.exchangedlife.com

ISBN: 978-0692576908

All rights reserved. No part of this book may be reproduced in any form or by any electronic or mechanical means including information storage and retrieval systems, without permission in writing from the author. The only exception is by a reviewer, who may quote short excerpts in a review.

Contact the author by visiting http://www.eddiesnipes.com or http://www.exchangedlife.com

Unless otherwise stated, the scripture in this book have been taken from the New King James Version. Copyright © 1982 by Thomas Nelson, Inc. Used by permission. All rights reserved.

Picture Credits
Front cover photo(s) purchased at:
http://www.dreamstime.com

Table of Contents

Introducing Your Victory 4
    Discussion Questions. 12
My Testimony of Deliverance 13
    Discussion Questions 25
Life Begins With Trust 26
    Discussion Questions 40
Overcoming Temptation 41
    Discussion Questions 55
Learning to Walk in the Spirit 57
    Discussion Questions 67
A Word for the Wives 68
Appendix A 75
Other Recent Books by Eddie Snipes 81

Introducing Your Victory

If you are defeated by a pornography addiction, you are part of a special group that is dear to God's heart – and much closer to God's purpose than you realize. The temptation that you think is destroying you is actually driving you to discover the special place in God's heart for those who struggle. Jesus revealed God's heart toward those who are downcast – including those with moral failures, and it wasn't the same response as that of religious leaders.

One day a prostitute came into a house where Jesus was dining with a religious ruler of Israel. Her bad reputation was well known in the city, and the men near Jesus were repulsed at this woman's entrance. She took an alabaster box of fragrant oil. It was an heirloom that represented her family inheritance, and was very costly. It was likely her most valuable possession.

She fell at Jesus' feet, and her tears poured out the pain of her heart and soul. She was as unclean as they come. As the tears washed over Jesus' feet, she wiped them with her hair.

The men in the room began whispering to one another. "If this Jesus were truly a prophet, he would know what manner of woman is touching him. She is a sinner." And by sinner, they meant that she was part of the gutters of society. In that culture, a religious leader would never allow a common sinner to touch him, much less this unclean town prostitute.

The woman with the tortured soul began to kiss Jesus' feet. Then she took the alabaster box, which was the equivalent of two years' worth of wages, and she broke it open and poured the perfumed oil on Jesus' feet.

It was her way of declaring, "I am completely broken, and I have nothing of value in my life. I'm laying my shattered life and all I have at your feet. You are my only hope."

Out of all the great men in her city, those esteemed with status, religious leadership, and unquestioned reputation, why did she come to Jesus? Religion and religious people condemn, but

Jesus never condemned. Jesus had a unique reputation. Though His character was unmatched by any, Jesus had no problem sitting at dinner with prostitutes, drunkards, and the dregs of society. Not one time does Jesus call those entrapped in sin a sinner. Not one time did Jesus ever condemn the sinner.

Sinners were drawn to this man, even though His life made theirs look shameful. His words never put them to shame, but every sinner recognized their condition when they encountered Jesus. The dishonest and thieving tax collector proves this. He was a man whose love of money had persuaded him to forfeit his reputation to pad his pockets. He had become extremely wealthy by inflating tax bills so he could pocket the extra. Zacchaeus was hated by his neighbors, and was pushed out of society.

When Jesus came to town, everyone shoved Zacchaeus to the back of the crowd. He had to climb a tree near the road where Jesus was walking, just to get a glimpse of this new kind of rabbi.

When Jesus passed, He stopped and said, "Zacchaeus, come down. I will dine with you today."

Oh the horror of such a social atrocity for anyone claiming to be a moral teacher! To dine with a sinner was an abomination. In that culture, to dine with someone was a declaration of acceptance and friendship. Though Jesus never condemned Zacchaeus, this former thief was touched by God and said, "I will pay back four times what I stole from any man by dishonesty, and then I'll give half of what's left to the poor."

He had captured a glimpse of the treasure of God's grace, and when he did, everything else seemed worthless. Without condemnation, he was drawn to repentance through the love of God.

When the foul-mouthed Peter caught a glimpse of the man of Grace, without any words of condemnation, he said, "Depart from me Lord, for I am a sinful man."

Instead of departing, Jesus welcomed Peter into His inner circle, and created an apostle out of a sinner.

This has always been God's plan. Even in the Old Testament, a sinful man named Isaiah encountered the Lord. When he saw the glory of the Lord, he said, "Woe to me, for I am undone. I am a man of unclean lips, and I live among a people of unclean lips."

God touched Isaiah and said, "I have purged your sins and taken away your iniquity." Then God gave His call for ministry in the hearing of Isaiah, and the man who had been focused on his sins moments before was now begging God to send him. Then God made a prophet out of the sinner.

No doubt the woman at Jesus' feet had been touched by grace. In the presence of such grace, her lifestyle of sin became worthless. She suddenly understood that Jesus held a treasure that she did not possess, and could never possess in her current state. The most prized possession she had was merely a reflection of her broken life. Just as her shattered life couldn't hold anything of true value, she broke her alabaster box and released the aroma of her life to the Lord. It is just as the Bible says in **Psalm 34:18**

> The LORD *is* near to those who have a broken heart, And saves such as have a contrite spirit.

The Bible reiterates this in **Psalm 51:17**
> The sacrifices of God *are* a broken spirit, A broken and a contrite heart-- These, O God, You will not despise.

Religion looked at the sinner and said, "She made her bed. Let her lie in it. This woman is not fit for the Lord."

But God looks at the sinner and says, "A broken spirit and crushed heart will *never* be despised." And this is what the word 'contrite' means. We are taught that we must focus on our sins and have contrition, but the word here is 'dakah' in the Hebrew, which means to be crushed, contrite, or to be shattered.

When the woman was pouring out her broken heart, Jesus asked her critics a question. "Who loves more, the one who is forgiven of fifty days wages, or the one forgiven of five-hundred days wages?" The man hosting the dinner correctly answered that the one forgiven of more will love more. Jesus then pointed out that the host had not done anything that expressed love toward

Christ, but the sinful woman expressed a heart filled with loving gratitude. He then concluded with **Luke 7:47-48**

> ⁴⁷ "Therefore I say to you, her sins, which are many, are forgiven, for she loved much. But to whom little is forgiven, *the same* loves little."
>
> ⁴⁸ Then He said to her, "Your sins are forgiven."

Do not take this as earning forgiveness. Jesus didn't say those who weren't showing love weren't forgiven. He said their sins were smaller so they would love less. The reason is because they couldn't recognize the value of the forgiveness being given to them. Also, the statement, "her sins, which are many, are forgiven, for she loved much," is not saying that her love merited her forgiveness.

The entire point of Jesus' explanation is that she loved more BECAUSE she understood she had been forgiven of many sins. The phrase 'for she loved much', can literally be translated as 'so that' she loved much. The Greek word translated here is the word 'hoti', which means because, so that, or that. She was forgiven of much, and that is why she loves much. Because of this she loves much.

When the Bible speaks of Jesus dining with prostitutes and drunkards, it does not say who these people were, but from this story we can see one of them. We're not given a glimpse into the previous encounter with this woman, but she had clearly been touched by grace. After being rejected by society for her moral failures, she was driven to show gratitude to the only person who had looked past her sins, and rescued her heart.

It's important to make this distinction, for if we lose sight of our love being a response to God's love, then we will make this into another religious requirement. We'll then fall into the trap of religion, which takes an illustration that shows us that God rescues us from sin, and will make it into something we must do in order to rescue ourselves from our sin.

Whether you are male or female, you are this woman. Your addiction to pornography has put you into the special group of people who are so broken in spirit that they can see how valuable God's love is. God does not want you to clean up your act in order to be received. He wants you to understand how much He loves you, and it's His job to clean up your life. Your job is to receive His loving kindness. His job is to transform your heart and restore you with true life.

The first step in recovery is to believe God's declaration of love over you. God is delighted when men and women with sin-filled lives put their trust in His love and mercy. There is only one barrier between God and you – unbelief. Not sin. Not a polluted mind. Not addictions. Not guilt, shame, or condemnation. If you disbelieve and put your trust in sin, that is erecting a barrier between you and receiving God's love. And love does not force itself upon those who reject it. However, if you believe, you will trust God enough to give Him your sins, so your newly emptied hands can receive the gift of God's love.

The sacrifice God accepts from you is a broken spirit and crushed heart. Rarely do I meet a man struggling with a sexual addiction that is not broken in heart and spirit. Not one Christian man I have met that is addicted to pornography wanted to be stuck in that addiction. When I was addicted, I hated porn. I hated my life. I hated what I had become. But I was powerless to control these overwhelming desires, and the church had no answers. Or perhaps I should say, the church had the wrong answers.

In the next chapter, I'll go into my experience. In this chapter I want you to understand that God loves you with a perfect love, and He delights in reaching into sin to rescue you. He is not angry with you. He is not seething with anger because you can't control yourself. He says, "Whoever believes on Christ will not be put to shame."[1]

The more you are filled with God's love, the more addictions are washed away. If someone had told me that God cleanses me with the power of His love through the Spirit, my journey would have been much different. Instead, feelings of condemnation drove me away from God, when I should have been drawn toward Him. I

---

[1] Romans 10:11

was given a false view of God. I was told that God rejected me in my sin, and no one told me that Jesus was a friend of sinners.[2]

As long as you believe your sin can defeat God's love, you will continue to struggle and fail. Once you believe that God's love for you is not based upon your character, but His character, you'll begin to grow in grace.

The Bible says, "It is the goodness of God that leads you to repentance."[3] The word 'repentance' means 'to change the mind.' It does not mean to grovel in sorrow, but to focus on God's goodness and allow it to transform your mind from a fleshly way of thinking, to an eternal way of thinking.

I am going to take you through the steps that I guarantee will lead you to a life without addiction and a mind cleansed from pornography. No book can change your life, but a book like this can provide a living testimony as proof that these principles work. It can provide you with the principles that, if applied, will change your life. But you must be willing to trust God, His word, and the power of His Spirit to accomplish what God has promised. You must learn to stop trusting in your weakened will, and put your trust in the promise of the Holy Spirit within you.

The Bible says that the same Spirit that raised Jesus from the dead dwells in you, and will give life to your physical body.[4] Raising the dead body of Christ is much more miraculous than your problem. Therefore, if God has the power to raise a dead body to life, it is no problem for God to raise you out of the corruption of sin, and revitalize you through the power of His Spirit that dwells within you.

This begins with believing that God loves you enough to take your sins. It takes trust to give God the sacrifice of your sinful life. Why do we put on a mask before our coworkers, church, friends, and family? We really don't trust them enough to let them see our faults. Often times, this is rightly so, for people are imperfect, and they make acceptance conditional.

---

[2] Matthew 11:19, Luke 7:34
[3] Romans 2:4
[4] Romans 8:11

When sharing how God delivered me from pornography, a man once said, "You aren't forgiven. When God gives someone over to a reprobate mind, He is writing them off, and the Bible says that there remains no more sacrifice for sin if we fall away." He rejected me and my testimony because it violated what he thought God should forgive and what he thought was unforgivable.

I said, "Apparently, someone forgot to tell God that He can't forgive me. It wasn't the devil that changed my life."

The Bible never says that a Christian who falls away can't be forgiven. This is a misinterpretation of a scripture that is taken out of context. I address this in another book, so I won't do that here. However, I will emphasize that man's acceptance is conditional, but every condition of godliness has been accomplished through Christ, and through Him, everything is a free gift received by faith. You are acceptable to God because you are in Christ. No other requirement is necessary. Any other requirement is a denial of what Christ has done.

Don't hide your sins from God. Don't run from God when you fail. You'll know you are learning to trust when you give God your sins instead of your righteousness. God gives you His righteousness in exchange for your sins. A disbelieving Christian can't trust God with their sins. This causes them to fall away from Him, instead of coming confidently to the throne of grace. This is where the Bible promises God's help and more grace in our time of need.[5]

The sacrifice that pleases God is your broken spirit, for Jesus said, "Blessed are those who are poor in spirit, for theirs is the Kingdom of Heaven." In your sinful state that has driven your spirit to despair, when you understand that you cannot make your spiritual life be what it should be, and you know you have failed miserably, yours is the Kingdom of Heaven!

Trust God with your broken and scrambled up life. This is the only gift you can give God which originates from you. A child that comes to their father with broken pieces and says, "I've ruined everything," is not rejected, but blessed. That's when God says, "Trust me with this," then He turns and drops it in the grave of

---

[5] Hebrews 4:16

Christ. He gives us a renewed spirit and says, "Now join me in the walk of faith, and let me show you what life in the Kingdom is all about."

God does not want your righteousness. He wants your sins, failures, corruption, and everything that hinders your life. That is your alabaster box. Break it at His feet and let the fragrance of His forgiveness fill your life. Then let the journey of faith begin!

Discussion Questions.

1. How has your addiction affected your life?

2. When you fall into your sinful addiction, have you been taught that God is angry, or that He is your friend?

3. Did Jesus require Zacchaeus, the dishonest tax collector, to get his life right before he could have fellowship with Christ?

4. Did Jesus tell Peter, the fisherman, to get his life right before inviting him to join Jesus' circle of disciples?

5. What caused the foul-mouthed Isaiah to recognize his sins?

6. What led the prostitute to come and pour her heart out at Jesus' feet?

7. Did Jesus tell her to break and pour out the alabaster box before she could be forgiven?

8. Why does the Bible say, "It is the goodness of God that leads you to repentance?

9. What did Jesus mean by, "Blessed are those who are poor in Spirit?"

10. Take a moment to give God the offering of your life, sins and all. Trust God with your sins, and ask Him to reveal to you His righteousness. Thank God for His grace, unmerited and undeserved favor. Take a moment to meditate on His love for you.

My Testimony of Deliverance

Zephaniah 3:17
>The LORD your God in your midst, The Mighty One, will save; He will rejoice over you with gladness, He will quiet *you* with His love, He will rejoice over you with singing.

For most of my life, I couldn't hear His song. It was drowned out by many well-meaning, but misguided teachers of the Bible.

"Examine your heart," I listened to the preacher proclaiming from the pulpit. "Look at your sin. Some of you have secret sin in your life! You can hide it from the church, but don't think you can hide it from God. Surely your sins will find you out."

I knew he was talking to me. Not one person in my life knew the internal war raging inside. I hated my sin. I hated my addiction to pornography. It had created a rollercoaster Christianity in me, with rare upswings and long downswings in my life.

"God is going to take you behind the woodshed," the preacher continued. "God is angry at the wicked everyday!"

I felt the angry stare of God. Judgment was coming, and there was nothing I could do about it.

"Repent of your sins," he continued.

Been there. Done that. I repented nearly every week. Often daily. At least I did unless I was still caught up in the storm of a porn binge. A month ago I had come out of a binge and felt rotten to the core. My life was filled with sin, and my mind corrupted with the images still echoing in my recent memory. I had promised God I would never indulge in porn again. That commitment lasted almost three weeks, which was long for me. But it was a tormented three weeks.

My desires were like a fog. When the fog rolled in, my thoughts were clouded, and the only thing I could think about was satisfying this insatiable hunger of my flesh. "No!" I had proclaimed. I would not do it this time. I resisted with all my might, but my thoughts were already being sucked into the fog. I had to be strong enough. I would defeat it this time. But it was like chains hooked into my brain. It was pulling, and though I fought against it, the fog pulled at my mind, beckoning with the song of the sirens.

One day, I decided to read my Bible and try to focus my thoughts on godliness. I lay across my bed, reading the scriptures. Then the fog rolled back in, this time with all its force. I could think of nothing but the call of the fog. I tried to continue reading, but all I was seeing was words in print, but no comprehension of their meaning. I was tired of the war. I was tired of fighting. And besides, if I wasn't safe from temptation when reading the Bible, where could I be safe?

My thoughts were dispelled by a loud proclamation from the preacher. "Did you know that one study said the average teenage boy thinks of sex once every eight seconds?" the preacher asked. He paused for effect while his eyes scanned the audience for guilty faces.

I wish I could have eight seconds of relief. Unless something required my undivided attention, my thoughts were always on lust. Every idle moment, my mind returned to the pit.

"Some of you have minds filled with corruption. God knows the thoughts of your heart. Your sin has separated you from the love of God," he said as he shook his finger to each section of the sanctuary.

That was me. I had been indulging in porn, and this was the first day I had emerged from the fog in at least a week. Yet even now, my thoughts had scarcely left the gutter, and had only peeked out at the sound of these words of condemnation. But I knew my mind was going back there when this sermon came mercifully to an end.

"You need to get your heart right with God," the preacher said as his finger scanned across the congregation, searching for sinners. He briefly stopped to poke the air when he detected sin in the camp.

His finger lowered to point to the carpeted steps on the platform. "Come down to this altar and repent! Get your life right with God." The finger pointed to the back door to emphasize his next words, "You aren't promised tomorrow. You might drive out of this parking lot and get hit by a Mac truck. Then you'll be standing before your Judge with sin on your hands. What will you do? What can you do?" He swept both arms out as if to fling the congregation out of his sight. "Nothing! There will be nothing you can do...because it's too late. You'd better get down here and repent. This might be your last chance!"

How many times had I heard this message? How many times had I responded with pleadings of mercy? The piano began playing as the congregation started singing *Just As I Am*. A few convicted souls began to go down. I felt my heart stiffen at the thought. For the last seventeen years I had been repenting of this great sin. I had promised God each time that I would never commit this sin again. Some weeks I fell a day or two later. Sometimes I fell before I could get home from church. One time I made it three whole months. It was a terrible three months, and it also ended in failure. I felt a moment of relief when the last line of the hymn ended. Now the reminder of my guilt could come to an end.

"I know God is convicting someone else in this room. This might be your last chance. Won't you come?" The congregation returned to the first stanza and sorrowfully sang, Just As I Am, giving one last opportunity for repentance.

Why am I bothering with this? God is angry with me, and even if I repent, in a few days I'll fall and He'll be more angry than before. I'm doomed anyway. For nearly two decades I've been in a constant state of either repentance or sinning. I'm either gnashing my teeth in misery trying not to sin, or I'm miserable knowing that I am sinning and incurring God's wrath.

Whether I repent or not, I am going to be under God's judgment because I cannot tame this beast within. Why come here every Sunday and be reminded of how angry God is with me? He's angry if I come, and He'll be angry if I don't come. At least if I don't come, I won't have to be constantly reminded of the doom that lies ahead – and cannot be avoided.

That was the day I cast my faith aside. I decided that the only way to have peace is to let my desires run their course, without the constant reminder of my impending judgment.

Someone who has not been overtaken by the fog of addiction does not understand. I recently had a man tell me about his brother with a sexual addiction. "I keep telling him that all he has to do is just stop doing it. How hard is that?"

It's much harder than you think.

During my time of growing out of pornography, I began to study the reasons behind such an addiction. I read a study about men with abnormal sexual cravings. Researchers discovered that the certain parts of the brain related to sexuality are larger in men with sexual addictions.

Also, during brain scans of men with sexual compulsions and addictions, three portions of the brain were significantly more active in men with sexual addictions than in men without addictions.

For those who want to research this topic, these are the ventral striatum, dorsal anterior cingulate, and the amygdala. The amygdala handles emotional and event processing. The ventral striatum is the reward center of the brain, which gives pleasure. The dorsal anterior cingulate is linked to the anticipation of rewards, and is responsible for cravings.

Studies have shown that these three areas of the brain in sexual addictions produce very similar responses as are seen in drug addictions. Some studies have suggested that the abnormal size of certain parts of the brain are linked to overstimulation during early childhood development. This means that a child exposed to sexual stimulation during development is likely to have a brain that has developed to excel in this way. In other words, early exposure is wiring you for addiction. It is possible to become addicted later in life, but most compulsive sexual addictions have their roots in pornography exposure, sexual abuse, or other early childhood sexual exposure.

My exposure began at the age of seven or eight. A childhood friend had an older brother at college. He had stored some boxes in my friend's room, and he discovered that there were hundreds of pornographic magazines in these boxes. He shared them with the boys of our neighborhood. We lived in a semirural area, so we built forts in the woods – the perfect hiding place for our magazines.

Each day, we'd visit our forts, swap magazines, and spend time flipping through the pages. This went on for years, and I never thought of it as being wrong – with one exception. Don't let our parents find out.

At the age of thirteen, I received Christ and something within me changed. It was the first time in my life that I felt pornography was wrong. When I looked at the magazines, I felt an inner struggle. I decided to stop visiting the magazines.

A few days later, I felt an overwhelming compulsion come over me. It was the first time I was swallowed by the fog. I couldn't think of anything except getting a fix from the magazines. For the next seventeen years, I went through hell. This was compounded by the message of condemnation being preached to me from the church.

I knew it was wrong, but my shame was being forged into guilt by the condemnation I was hearing each week. I expected to just stop, but when I tried, I entered into a world of near-insanity. I couldn't concentrate on anything when the craving hit. I had no power to resist – at least not for long. The longer I held out, the worse my mind fogged. My mind screamed for relief, and until I provided it, my concentration would not return.

When I married, I found that normal intimacy did not satiate my cravings. Now I had to hide my addiction from my wife, which meant I had to lie a lot. The more I lied to cover the trail of pornography, the more I became a liar in other areas. I couldn't keep my secret life in a box.

My marriage was stressed by the lack of honesty and secrecy. Though my wife didn't know about the pornography, she had a lot of mistrust and suspicion. When I swore off church, she saw my loss of interest in spiritual things, and complained that I wasn't being a spiritual leader to the family.

I thought that I would find relief by forgetting about God and letting my desires take their course. I didn't pray, read the Bible, or even think about the Lord for three to four years. Instead of making me happy, things grew worse. The craving could not be satisfied, and I never had peace in sin. I tried to drown out my lack of peace with more pornography, but after every indulgence, I felt empty, unsatisfied, and an inner conflict I didn't understand.

Not one idle minute passed without my mind being on sexual things. I could not sleep at night unless I allowed my mind to think on sexual lust. But nothing brought me rest.

The only way I could get my mind off porn was to concentrate on something else. So I poured myself into career development. I set a five-year goal. I wanted to become a certified MCSE engineer and land a job in server management. In between porn binges, I studied, worked, and earned certifications. A short time later, I landed the career I had set my sights on five years earlier. I had arrived!

That was the beginning of my internal collapse. I pursued and laid hold of everything I thought would make me happy, but I felt emptier than at any point in my life. It was as if I had climbed the mountain of success, only to find out nothing was up there.

I contemplated setting a higher goal, but as I reflected I realized, if nothing was on top of this mountain, nothing would be on top of the next mountain either. That realization sent me into a hopeless tailspin.

What I didn't realize was that God was setting me up for a greater purpose. According to what I had always heard, God turns his back when we sin, but instead of judgment, I found blessing and success — though these were meaningless outside of the relationship He created me to have with Himself. It was as if God was saying, "If you think these things will make you happy, try and see." I indulged in pornography without restraint and without a thought of God, and it brought me emptiness. I poured my life into my career, gained the success I was looking for, but it was worthless.

Looking back I can now see that God was not dealing with me according to my sins, but according to His goal for my life. A goal that could not be realized until pornography was out of the way. Yet He still was guiding my steps, setting me up for the blessed life He had planned. He did not wait for me to get it right. He prepared the way for the day when He would make all things right. Instead of judging me, God was leading me into the abundant life! He is the opposite of what I have been taught.

During my first week at my new job, I was in my office waiting for a project to start. I had several days free and was told to work on anything I wanted to focus on. It was an opportunity to start my next career path. But I couldn't concentrate. My life was meaningless. Porn ruled my life, but it provided nothing for all my expense and effort. It left me empty. My career had no real value. I had a larger paycheck, but what was the purpose? How could I continue to invest my life in something that was as empty as my starving soul?

Having freedom to come and go while waiting for a project, I left work and took a walk in a nearby park. I knew of no other option than to try to call out to the Lord I had abandoned nearly four years earlier. I spent the afternoon walking in the woods, sorting through my thoughts, and complaining to God. Nothing happened. After several hours, I left the park, still feeling as hopeless as before.

The next day, I still couldn't concentrate on studying. Part of me wanted to go back to the park, while another part of my mind thought, what's the use? God was drawing me, but my life was too crowded and confused to hear Him. But I could feel enough of His drawing to compel me to go back to the park and try to pray. I spent another day beating the air with the fist of my complaining, until I tired of it and went home.

I felt compelled to go back the following day, too. I walked and complained to God. I remember saying, "God, I can't do it. I can't live this Christian life. I can't stop these desires from taking over my mind. I can't beat this thing."

At my lowest and most sinful state, the time when I had abandoned God and even got to the point where I questioned His existence, God showed me His unmerited favor. If anyone was worthy of wrath, it was me, but God poured His Spirit into my life. My despair fled when a cloud engulfed me.

Though the day was sunny, a cloud fell on me and the woods disappeared. I felt God wash through my mind and heart, cleansing me of this plague of addiction. It felt like chains fell from my mind and scriptures came to mind that I don't remember knowing. One was Isaiah 61:10, "I will greatly rejoice in the Lord, my soul shall be joyful in my God; for He has clothed me with the garments of salvation, he has covered me with the robe of righteousness."

Then the Lord spoke into my heart, "To him who does not work, but believes on Him who justifies the ungodly, his faith is accounted for righteousness."

Time lost relevance, and I don't know whether I was in His presence five minutes or two hours. Many other scriptures came to mind that day, and before the cloud departed, the Lord gave me a challenge: Go and prove this with the scriptures.

I walked out of the woods a free man. I rushed home, found a concordance, and began looking up keywords to find the scriptures. Each word spoken to me was found in the Bible, and I found affirmation for the work God had just accomplished in my heart.

The fog of addiction was gone, but the flesh was strong. I had spent more than twenty years of my life feeding my flesh, and I had a long road to learn how to live according to the Spirit. The Bible promises that if we walk in the Spirit, we will not fulfill the lusts of the flesh.[6] Since I had no one to disciple me, it took many years to realize this truth.

This book will share what I discovered over the next eighteen years, as I learned how to escape the lure of pornography. There was no one who knew how to guide me. Many failures discouraged me and many people condemned me. What would have happened if someone had taught me what I'm about to share in this book?

---

[6] Galatians 5:16

When I first started sharing my experience, I got a lot of negative feedback. People told me that I wasn't saved. Others told me that I could never be forgiven. People misapplied many scriptures that seemed to heap condemnation upon me, but something in my spirit kept encouraging me to press on. How could I be unforgivable if God had done this for me? Would God surround someone He despised with the cloud of His embrace? Would God, who already knew my future, have wasted His time if my future struggles were putting me back under condemnation?

For many years I shared my testimony on a very limited basis. It wasn't welcomed in the churches I was involved in, but recently the Lord has shown me it was now His timing to use this experience so others can know His power to rescue them.

Looking back, I don't think I could have accurately shared this work of God, for I was being drawn out of a legalistic mindset, and did not fully understand how this applies to others with similar struggles. God used the criticism of others to restrain me until His work was more complete.

Your experience of deliverance may or may not be the same as mine. Don't think you have to see a cloud to find deliverance. The Apostle Paul hated Christians and fought against the church during the years shortly after Christ. His life was changed when God blinded him with a great light from heaven. He encountered Christ there, but that wasn't his message to others. His testimony convinced him of the power of God, but he never pointed others to his own experience, but to the reality of Jesus Christ.

Likewise, my testimony is how God worked in my life, but it's not my individual experience that is important. It was how God intervened in my life so He could focus me on the reality of His power to transform lives. In truth, it was the next eighteen years that truly unveiled God's work available to all, not the wilderness experience I had.

After my rescue, I didn't know how to translate my testimony into something others can draw from. Many years ago, when sharing with a man who was struggling, he asked, "Why doesn't God do this for me? How do I find the same victory?"

It was a question I couldn't answer at the time, but now I have a clearer perspective. Part of this perspective came through working my way through the struggles of a mind that was called into the life of faith, but knew nothing but lust.

Though the fog of compulsive desires never came back, I did find myself struggling with lust once the emotions of relief faded. I had to work through the battle of falling into lust and how that affected my relationship with God. I had to support equipment in a store in a mall. I remember walking through the mall saying to myself, "Don't look. Don't look. Don't look." I had to walk past two lingerie shops with seductive displays. Several teen shops had seductive ads. The perfume counter had sexuality everywhere. Ads hanging from the ceiling had scantily clad women on the poster. It was everywhere. Sometimes those things would trigger that old desire, and I'd be tempted to return to the world of sensuality.

The other day I had to walk through a mall and found myself face to face with a sexy ad. It was then that I realized how great a work God has done in my life. It hit me that I've walked by those same temptations and not once did I think, "Don't look." I didn't think about it at all.

I have a friend whose husband was miserable on a cruise ship. He said the women in skimpy attire made his life difficult. Another friend mentioned a relative that was angry for going on an outing where he was faced with women in seductive swimwear. He was angry because he felt like the family put him in temptation's way.

Having been there I know what these men are going through. They are trying to walk in godliness, but lust overthrows their minds. There is a good chance these men struggle with pornography.

When I went on an anniversary cruise with my wife, I was a little concerned after hearing about the attire the women often wear, but I had no problems. I look back and realize what a miracle this is. Where my mind once was entrapped by every sexual temptation, now rarely does a thought pass by. And when it does, I can rest in the confidence of God's power to defeat every temptation.

My prayer is that you experience the same life of victory. Instead of being overrun by temptation, you can stand in confidence with the Lord. Instead of focusing on not looking, I pray you look up one day and say, "What happened to the temptation?"

When a toddler learns to walk, it's usually a steady process. They first stand while holding onto something. They hold their parent's fingers while walking. But then they let go and take a step. Then they fall. Their parents don't scold them, but praise them. "Good job! You took a step."

Then they take a couple of steps and fall. Over time, the steps get longer and the falls get fewer. When they begin, they are focused on making that one step. A toddler just learning to walk watches their feet, puts out their arms to balance, and their focus is on not falling. But as walking becomes second nature, they don't even think about falling. They don't even think about walking. Their thoughts are on where they are going.

Now let me ask you a question. Are you a better parent than God? Do you naturally encourage your young children as they struggle to learn to walk, but God beats His children who are struggling to walk? Absolutely not!

God is a better parent than any of us could ever be. Yet, we have painted a terrible picture of God so that people are afraid to step out in faith. When someone falls, we tell them God is angry. Not so! God is cheering you on, telling you to keep your trust in His love. Arise and take that next step!

Rare is the person who recovers without a struggle. It happens, but rarely. We feel God drawing us out of the flesh, and we are completely dependent upon His upholding hand. He is giving us strength and calling us to step out. When you fall, God picks you up with His hand and says, "Good job! Now get up and start again. Learn to look at Me and you won't fall."

You'll do well for a while and then the tempter will come around to distract you. You'll fall. Then the tempter will say, "God is angry. You're a disappointment to God."

This is a lie. It's time to start believing what God says about Himself, and stop listening to what others say about Him. If you learn to trust in His love for you, instead of running from Him or groveling in defeat, you'll keep moving forward with expectation. Expect to see God do the miraculous. Persevere. The only thing that will defeat you is disbelief in His love and acceptance for you. If you learn to walk in faith, the time will come when you'll stop thinking 'don't fall', and you'll look up one day and say, "What happened to my weakness? What happened to the temptation that once seemed so strong?"

As you go forward, read with expectation. God's desire is to show Himself strong on your behalf. He wants you to be strong in Him – not in your own strength. God has created us with what seems like flaws, but are actually empty places in our lives that are designed for Him alone. If you try to make yourself strong, you are missing the revelation of God in you. Temptation is how we try to fill the empty places, but nothing fits. Our empty places are designed for Him.

As you learn to trust in God, you'll find that as He fills your life, temptation is pushed out of your life, for it has no gap to sneak into. And this is the underlying principle of this book. I want you to see how to trust in God's love, promises, and the true abundant life. The more you walk in God's love, the more your life is transformed, and the more weaknesses are eliminated.

Prayerfully read this book knowing that it is God's desire to make you complete in Him, and abundantly satisfied in Him. Then watch the addiction fade into the distant past.

Discussion Questions

1. Why do our churches focus more on sin than on God's deliverance from sin?

2. What happens when we have the expectation of God's wrath? Do we come to Him or run from Him?

3. After reading my testimony, did you see God's anger or love and grace?

4. When you struggle or fall, do you feel like God is angry at you?

5. Write out your testimony or speak about it. How did your addiction begin?

6. Do you think God would send people to you to testify of His love unless His purpose was to do the same with you?

7. Why do you think your efforts to break free have failed in the past?

8. Read Romans 5:8. Does God love sinners?

9. Read Romans 5:9-10. If God loved you before you received Christ, does His love increase or decrease when you struggle now?

10. Do you feel loved by God?

Life Begins With Trust

The single most important thing in experiencing the abundant life promised to us by God is trust. If you can't trust God's promise that your righteousness comes through the power of the Spirit working in you, then you'll disbelieve when you see your mistakes. Spiritual maturity is not dependent upon you. Acceptance with God is not dependent upon you. The only thing required is faith – your willingness to believe what God has said, and trust in Him.

The Bible says that we are accepted because we are in the Beloved, which is Christ.[7] When explaining how we are overcomers in Christ,[8] the Bible says it is because we have known and believed in the love God has for us.[9]

If you can't trust in God's love for you, you will never experience the full life of the Spirit God has given to every Christian. Your sin is not the problem. Faith is the problem. Before doing His work in someone's life, Jesus often said, "Be it according to your faith."

When Jesus visited His hometown, they scoffed at His power, and the Bible says, "He did not do many mighty works there because of their unbelief."[10] It was not their sins, nor was it a lack of religious effort. Unbelief is the only hindrance in the Christian life. The Bible warns us to beware that we don't have an evil heart of unbelief, which causes us to depart from the living God.[11]

Why didn't the Bible say that sin causes us to depart? It is because the only limitation God has placed on Himself in our lives is faith. God will not violate your trust. He will honor what you choose to put your trust in.

Faith is God's invitation to enter into His mighty works as He reveals them to us. Through His word and through the revelation

---

[7] Ephesians 1:6
[8] 1 John 4:4
[9] 1 John 4:16
[10] Matthew 13:58
[11] Hebrews 3:12

of Himself to us in the Spirit, God invites us to believe Him. Once we believe, we receive. Once we disbelieve, we have shunned the promise and will remain in the flesh.

The real question is, do you trust in sin's power more than God's power? Stop worrying about sin. Sin is God's problem, not yours. Your addiction is not your problem, but it's also God's problem. Unbelief is your problem.

You can't overcome sin by focusing on sin. Addiction is the flesh's dependence on a destructive behavior, which is a form of sin. So in the same way, you can't overcome addiction by focusing on your addiction. Addiction is not your identity – it is the result of being underdeveloped spiritually, or spiritual immaturity.

The reality of life is that the vast majority of the sins you commit will never even make it into your conscious mind. Let me give an example. If someone says something thoughtless to you or about you, it is hurtful. Is their offense to you a sin? Sure it is. Anytime we hurt someone, we have committed a wrong. Yet, most of the time that person shrugs off our offense as no big deal.

It makes us angry and frustrated, yet we do the same thing. When someone gets upset over something we see as petty, our response is, "What's their problem?" Since our feelings are not affected and we can't see their perspective, we don't think we have wronged them. So we can see when we are offended, but not when we offend others. That's human nature.

What about when we let someone down? Or what about when we make a promise with good intensions, but life gets in the way and we break our word? The Bible even tells us that whatever is not of faith is sin.[12] Have you ever taken any action without the absolute assurance that you are walking in God's work and provision? Certainly you have. We all have.

The reason to bring this up is to show that every person has sin. We only recognize the big things that capture our attention. Think back when you were a teenager (or if you have children, think of their behavior). Is a teen selfish? Do they act with maturity? Sometimes they do, but many times they do not. When a child

---

[12] Romans 14:23

throws a fit, is that a mature way of acting? Why do kids have fits? They are living in selfishness, and their behavior emerges from a childish way of thinking. Now consider **1 Corinthians 13:11**

> When I was a child, I spoke as a child, I understood as a child, I thought as a child; but when I became a man, I put away childish things.

A child doesn't stop acting childish because someone tells them they are foolish. They grow out of childish behavior. A normal adult doesn't go into a daycare, look around to see if an adult is watching, and sneak toys by putting them into their pocket. Why are they not tempted? It's because they are not in that old mindset. A four-year-old will try to sneak a toy out because they are thinking like a four-year-old.

As a young teen, I took many foolish risks and acted out in many foolish ways that I would never consider doing today. Why? Because my way of thinking has matured, and now that old way seems worthless.

In the same way, an immature Christian will act in many unChrist-like ways. A young Christian has many beliefs and actions that will one day seem very foolish. Like the Bible says above, we speak like children and act like children, but when we mature, we put away those childish things.

Sin is a childish way of thinking. When we are spiritual children, we are blind to our own sin. In fact, many of our childish sins will never be recognized. We'll simply leave them behind. Others will be obvious sins to us as we mature.

I quit playing with action figures when my personal maturity became incompatible with my old childish way of playing. No one had to tell me to stop playing with the old toys, I naturally graduated away from them. This is why the church often teaches from the wrong perspective. We scold immature Christians for acting in immature ways, when the answer is to mature them out of fleshly/childish ways of thinking.

This is how I overcame many of the life-issues that haunted me. When I had anger issues, it was because I wanted life to revolve around my expectations. When they weren't met, I became selfishly angry. What I thought was a wrong done to me was actually a wrong way of thinking on my part. But as I matured, I grew to realize that I was being self-centered. My anger dissipated when I began thinking differently.

When trying to overcome lust, I did not understand these things. I tried to make myself resist my desires, instead of growing into a better way of thinking, which has better desires. I no longer make myself stop looking for lust. I have a better and healthier desires that lust robs me of experiencing. The more I grew spiritually, the more those old desires became incompatible with the man I was growing into. Then like the childish toys I put away because I stopped enjoying them, I stopped pursuing temptation because it was no longer enjoyable. It was robbing me of experiencing the more enjoyable life in the Spirit.

The flesh is the childish way of thinking. The life of the Spirit is where we are going, and what we are growing into. The greater maturity you have in the Spirit, the more incompatible the life of the flesh becomes. Keep in mind that the Spirit's desires are against the flesh, and the flesh's desires are against the Spirit. These two are opposed to one another.[13] If you grow into spiritual maturity, the fleshly way of thinking and acting begins to look both foolish and unappealing.

If you try to overcome your addictions without growing in the Spirit, your success is very limited, and frustration will undermine your success. It's hard to overcome by resisting what you want. True recovery happens when you stop desiring what once captured your affections.

Once, I was approached with the offer to be published if I would revamp my addiction account, and take away the Christian content to make it appealing in the secular market. I declined because the things I am teaching can only work if someone desires to live in the Spirit. Keep this in mind as you go forward. This isn't a self-help book. It's an invitation to experience the life of the Spirit, where all God's power is limitless. If someone does not want to live

---

[13] Galatians 5:17

in the new life God has given through Christ, this book cannot help you. If someone is stuck in the religious mindset where they only believe God helps those who can repent well enough to get Him to act, this book can't help you. Of course, religion that is dependent upon your efforts can't help you either.

Contrary to what you may have heard, God is not offended by our sin. God is offended at what sin is doing to us. In fact, He's so offended that He came in the likeness of sinful flesh, and on account of sin, He went to the cross to condemn sin in His own flesh,[14] and in Christ, He conquered sin.[15] Sin does not have the power to keep you from God. The heart of the issue is that sin is filling a void in your life that was designed by God for God.

Sin only fills the places of vacuum in our soul. What religion has done is to tell people they need to get sin out of their lives so God can come in. This is false. It is the complete opposite of the truth. The truth is that when the Spirit of God fills our lives, sin cannot remain. It is driven out.

I like to compare this to trying to get darkness out of a room. Put someone in a dark room with a broom and tell them to sweep the darkness out. Not even a fool would try to do this, yet religion is doing this very thing, but disguising it with religious terminology. The devil loves religion, for it distracts and condemns. The real answer is to turn the light on. Darkness is the absence of light, and it cannot challenge light. In the same way, sin is the absence of the Spirit. Sin disappears when the Spirit fills our life. But sin can never drive the Spirit out. It only exists in the empty places where we have excluded the Spirit.

This is why the Bible tells us to be filled with the Spirit and to walk in the Spirit. The closer we grow in our fellowship with God, the more His presence fills our life. And the more sin must flee.

Religion is telling is to push sin out of our lives, which leaves a vacuum. God doesn't get sucked into the void. Temptation does. This is why I spent nearly two decades driving pornography out of my life, and pushing against it until all my strength was expended.

---

[14] Romans 8:3
[15] 1 Corinthians 15:56-57, 1 Peter 2:24

The moment I tired of working against the vacuum, the old sins flooded back in, greater than before.

In Matthew 12:43, Jesus tells an interesting story. When an unclean spirit goes out of a man, he goes through dry places looking for rest. Then he returns and finds the man's life cleaned up, swept, and put into order – but empty. Then he takes many spirits, worse than himself and returns, leaving that man in a worse state than before.

This is religion in a nutshell. It tells us what we should get out. Religion can even do its work to clean up someone's life. It gets people cleaned up and set in order. But because the person is empty, sin will return. We might substitute one addiction for another, or go back to the old addiction. Jesus' illustration fit my life very well. Each victory was followed by a return of pornography, but each time I didn't go back to only the old, but I continued to slide deeper into the pit. Temptation grew stronger, the desires were harder to satisfy, and greater wickedness called me to cross more and more lines.

The reason you cannot overcome is because you cannot empty your life of sin and expect it to stay empty. The reason we are tempted to begin with is because we have a need in our life that temptation promises to fill. Where there is no need, there is no response to temptation.

In John chapter 4, Jesus goes to a well to encounter a woman in great need. There was a deep need in her life, and she believed she could fill it with relationships. She was obviously needy, for she went from man to man, trying to find someone who would fulfill her needs. She married and divorce five times. Yet, no one could fill the void in her heart. She was now living with a man who was not her husband.

If you read this chapter, take note that Jesus did not begin with her problem, but the true need. He began telling her about the living water of the Spirit, that once it was flowing in her life, the thirst would be gone. When her sinful lifestyle came up, Jesus did not condemn her sins, but invited her and her companions to come and discover the living water.

Jesus used hunger and thirst as the needs of our life with the promise that if we direct our hunger toward righteousness, we will be filled.[16] The real need is not physical, but spiritual. Even in this, religion tells us we must become righteous, but God declares that righteousness is His gift to us. It is His righteousness we hunger for, not our own.[17] When we are feeding and having our thirst quenched by His righteousness, the need gives way to abundance. Where there once was a need, becomes a river of living water that flows out to others. That is the power of the Spirit.

Sin is not your problem. Sin is the symptom of your problem. If you treat the symptoms, the underlying problem will never be cured. In fact, your condition will worsen.

A couple of generations back, scurvy and rickets were serious diseases that plagued some people. The diseases were not the problem, but the symptom of a problem. The problem was lack. Sailors on long voyages would often get scurvy because they only carried foods with a long shelf-life. They weren't taking in Vitamin C. As their bodies became more and more famished for this vital nutrient, their disease would worsen.

The same is true for rickets. It was misdiagnosed for many years because people didn't realize it was caused by a lack of calcium, or a lack of Vitamin D, which helps the body absorb calcium. No matter how much they treated the symptoms of the sickness, they could not recover. The solution was to nourish the body with what it needed.

Lacking in spiritual nutrition is the problem of your starving soul. The weakness of temptation is merely the symptom of a diseased soul. It's a disease of lack. How is it that someone who eats junk food can be grossly obese, yet starving for food? Sometimes it is an emotional starvation, but it is also a nutritional deficiency. They are gaining a lot of calories, but no nutrition. So their bodies keep sending out signals to be fed, and because they remain on a diet that can't supply the need, they overindulge but are never satisfied.

---

[16] Matthew 5:6
[17] Romans 5:17, 2 Corinthians 5:21

A starving soul indulges in sin, but because sin cannot satisfy, the hunger is rarely satiated. Our flesh demands satisfaction, and because the only thing we know is the junk food of the soul, we continue to feed this to our minds until we are sick of consuming. We may supplement our diet with spiritual things, but if it is spiritual junk food, this also leaves us famished.

You were not created for religion. You were created for intimacy with God, and being filled with the Spirit is the only thing that can satisfy your cravings. A soul that is starving will readily consume any temptation placed before it. That temptation fades as we learn true satisfaction. Look at the words of **Proverbs 27:7**

A satisfied soul loathes the honeycomb, but to a hungry soul every bitter thing *is* sweet.

Pornography is bitter. All we must do is look at the end result. We lose self-respect, remain empty, feel discontented, not to mention all the consequences that surround both the industry, and the ones who consume it. Yet because we are starving, it seems sweet.

Why do homeless people dig through garbage dumpsters and eat what they find without any thought of its contamination, but at the buffet line in a restaurant, people are picky eaters?

When my soul was starving, I could not resist consuming pornography at every opportunity. When I finally understood that grace was the expression of God's love and acceptance of me, then I began to dine on the things that truly satisfied my soul. Then when temptation came around, I began to loathe it. I didn't want it because I recognized that I would have to step out of what satisfied my life in order to consume what nearly starved me to death.

I didn't start by hating pornography. I started discovering the life of the Spirit, and then God began to transform my desires from the empty things of the flesh, to the enriching things of the Spirit.

This is why your addiction can be a blessing. Because the symptoms of your starving soul cannot be hidden, it forces you to face the real problem. Those whose symptoms are easy to overlook remain undiagnosed, and never have a great enough need to drive them to the abundant life God has given to all people. The symptoms don't disappear immediately, but as spiritual health emerges, the symptom of addiction weakens.

In the beginning, I still rummaged through the dumpsters of pornography, because I was conditioned to think like a fleshly person. But as I became more satisfied in Christ, I began losing my taste for temptation.

Jesus alluded to this when He spoke of new wineskins. He explained that the life of the Spirit was the new wine, but the old life we had is the old wineskin. It is too weak to contain the new wine, so we must be first made new and then we can possess the new wine of the Spirit. Yet, after this Jesus made an interesting statement, "No one having drunk the old wine immediately desires the new, for they say, 'The old is better.'"[18]

This is why we shouldn't be too hard on ourselves or other carnally minded Christians. At first, a new Christian thinks the old is better. It's not until we start being filled with the new life that we realize the new is better. The old mindset desires the taste of the old life. It's only when we begin developing the new life that our taste changes, and we realize the old is actually wine that has gone bad.

And this is an important lesson. Religion will beat you down for revisiting the dumpster, but this is not what happens under God's grace. Grace keeps inviting us to dine and the banquet table and eat freely. When I was stuck in the religious mindset, I believed my sins disqualified me from the banquet table. This was a ploy of the enemy to keep me in defeat. As I learned that God's acceptance was unconditional, I began dining on the life of the Spirit, and the life of the flesh slowly faded from view.

I say that God's acceptance is unconditional, but there is one condition. We are accepted because we are in Christ. Once I became a new creation and child of God, I became accepted by God. My acceptance is based on Christ's acceptance. My sins did not overthrow the success of Christ. Sin is not greater than Jesus; therefore, my failure does not equate to Jesus' failure.

---

[18] Luke 5:39

Religion uses shame, guilt, and condemnation as instruments of punishment to keep us out of sin. But it doesn't work. When our hunger grows greater than our will or our fear, we will return to sin.

What religion and most churches don't seem to recognize is that because we have a new spirit (which was given to us when we answered the call of faith) that spirit has the same desires as God, for it is a partaker of God's divine nature.[19] Just as the flesh hungered for lust and the things of the flesh, our new nature hungers for God's righteousness and the things of the Spirit.

False teaching focuses on the flesh. Look at your sin. You need to be more righteous. You need to be holy. You need to do more for God. You need to give more. You need to love God more.

True teaching focuses on Christ. Look at His righteousness, His holiness, His love for you. True teaching believes God's promise that He gives us a new spirit, puts His Spirit within us, takes away our desire for the flesh, and He will cause us to walk in His ways.[20] It's all about Him.

Because we have a new spirit, there is always a hunger for holiness, for we long to be nearer to God. And holiness is not our lack of sin, but our closeness to God. So to help people outgrow sin, we must teach them how to see God's invitation to come. No one matures out of sin by being scolded and by using fear tactics. As each person matures in the faith, the things that are incompatible with where they are going will be left behind.

Let me reiterate this important truth. You will outgrow sin as you grow into the faith. Therefore, your focus should be on growing in the faith and not on trying to force yourself to stop doing what the immature flesh craves.

There are indeed consequences to sin, but living life to avoid consequences is not the abundant life. Learning what manner of life you have been given, and exploring the richness of your life in Christ is the abundant life.

The truth is that no Christian can have peace or rest in sin. Every Christian, regardless of how carnal they are, has an inner

---

[19] 1 Peter 1:4
[20] Ezekiel 36:26-27

desire for holiness. Each Christian, no matter what sinful pattern they are stuck in, has a hunger for righteousness. Teachers, preachers, and church leaders should be appealing to that inner life of the Spirit instead of beating on the outer life of the flesh.

If you don't feel the need for righteousness and the desire to be holy, I recommend taking a few moments to read Appendix A. This is where I go into how to become a Christian and what it means to trust in Christ.

Equally important is that if you have that inner longing, don't allow the enemy to cause you to disbelieve in God's love and acceptance of you, or believe you don't have, or have lost your salvation. Addiction to sin is not the evidence that you are not saved. It's the evidence that you are walking according to the flesh, but it doesn't mean you don't have the Spirit.

Even during my darkest days, the time when I abandoned church and decided to leave my faith behind, I never could completely sell out to sin. I could never completely forget God. I always wondered why I would have times in my life where I felt like getting things right with God. I was miserable because I couldn't be at peace in sin. I never had rest in my spirit, and try as I might, that inner need for holiness could not be snuffed out.

As you begin this journey of recovery, never lose sight that you are always accepted by God if you have received Christ. God's righteousness is His gift to you. Sin does not nullify God's gift, for the Bible says that the gifts and calling of God are irrevocable.[21]

And the most important truth is that God's love for you is because He is love. He loves you because that is who God is. His love is not conditional on what we have or haven't done. The Bible says that if God demonstrated his love for us while we were sinners (without Christ), how much more, having been justified by His blood, we shall continue to be saved from wrath through Him (Christ).[22]

In 1 Corinthians 13, the Bible describes God's love (agape) with the following attributes: agape suffers long (with patience

---

[21] Romans 11:29
[22] Romans 5:8-9

toward us), is kind, does not seek its own, is not provoked, thinks no evil, endures all things, bears all things, and most importantly, love/agape never fails.

God does not want you to get right for Him. He wants you to trust in the transforming power of the Spirit through His love. He wants to be glorified through taking your broken life, and making you a treasured trophy of His grace.

Never believe the lie that your addiction causes God to reject you. God will never disown you. God has said that even if we are faithless, He remains faithful, for He cannot deny Himself. Since you are a new creation that is part of Himself (for you are in Christ and Christ in you), you can no longer be denied. Let's conclude with a wonderful scripture from **1 John 4:16-19**

> [16] And we have known and believed the love that God has for us. God is love, and he who abides in love abides in God, and God in him.
> [17] Love has been perfected among us in this: that we may have boldness in the day of judgment; because as He is, so are we in this world.
> [18] There is no fear in love; but perfect love casts out fear, because fear involves torment. But he who fears has not been made perfect in love.
> [19] We love Him because He first loved us.

If you are in fear – especially the fear of judgment for your sins or addictions, you have not been made perfect in God's love. And it isn't about your love for God, but knowing and believing in His love for you.

The reason God gives you His righteousness instead of demanding righteousness from you is because of His love for you. His love doesn't seek itself, but seeks to lift you. The reason God doesn't demand holiness is because of His love for you. He wants you to be holy by allowing Him to draw you close to Him.

From this point on, I want you to stop confessing the power of sin. The Bible says to hold fast to the confession of our confidence, which is Jesus Christ. And since the Bible says we are the righteousness of God in Christ, it's time to stop calling yourself an addict. Forget the 12-Step mindset that says, "I am an addict." Start the grace-step mindset and begin confessing, "I am the righteousness of God in Christ."

When you blow it, and your sober mind returns to you, look up and thank God for His amazing gift of grace that is dependent upon Christ and not you, and say, "I thank you that I am the righteousness of God in Christ."

Every time you sin, obey God's command to come confidently before His throne of grace to find help in your time of need.[23] When you fail, God favors you. That's what grace means, God's undeserved favor toward you. Come before His throne of favor to find extra favor from God that will give you help when you are in need – which is when you have blown it.

Believe that God accepts you for no other reason than you have received His grace through Christ.

Believe that God loves you for no other reason than the fact He is love.

Believe that His love has the power to transform you. If you disbelieve anything, disbelieve this: do not believe in your ability to change or earn any favor with God. Disbelieve that your sins or weaknesses have the power to overthrow the work of Christ or the love of God. Disbelieve the lie that God's acceptance is conditional.

Remember, without faith it is impossible to please God. For we must believe God is who He said He is, and He is a rewarder of those who diligently seek Him.[24] The Bible puts one condition upon you – faith in the complete work of Christ. Faith is not a work. Faith is believing in God's work, and that convinces us to let go of ourselves, and receive the gifts of God's favor.

Don't listen to messages of condemnation. To the Christian, there is now no condemnation because we are in Christ.[25] Any message that creates fear is not of God, for the Lord has declared

---

[23] Hebrews 4:16
[24] Hebrews 11:6
[25] Romans 8:1, 9

that any who believe in His love for them will have no fear – even in the Day of Judgment.

Spend time reviewing and memorizing passages that affirm this truth. Once you understand God's acceptance, then you will have a heart to receive the promises that bring you into a life of recovery. Even when you struggle, you are the righteousness of God in Christ!

Discussion Questions

1. How does unbelief in God's promises cause us to fall into temptation?

2. How does unbelief in God's love and acceptance cause us to struggle more with addictions and other temptations?

3. Review 1 Corinthians 13:11. How does this apply to your life?

4. Is God's plan for us to stop sinning so we can grow spiritually? Or that spiritual growth matures us out of sin? Explain your answer.

5. How does spiritual growth weaken lustful desires?

6. Why did God create us with an emptiness in our hearts?

7. Explain the difference between fighting our addictions, and filling our life with the Spirit.

8. Explain what it means to say, "Where there is no need, there is no response to temptation?"

9. Review Proverbs 27:7. Why does your soul crave the bitter fruit of pornography?

10. If we have been given a new nature, born of God, what will happen to our desires if we live our lives focused on the new life of faith?

11. Read 1 Corinthians 13:4-7. This is a description of the love of God. Review the attributes of God's love and explain how His love endures when you fail.

12. Review 1 John 4:16-19. In verse 19, is the power of love based on our love for Him, or His love for us?

13. What happens to fear when a Christian rests in God's love? Does their weaknesses defeat God's love?

14. In Christ, are you an addict?

15. Explain what it means to come boldly before the throne of grace for help when you are in need.

Overcoming Temptation

Weakness is a gift, not a curse. Don't buy into the misconception that you must be strong enough to overcome temptation. After many failures, I promised God that I would resist temptation and try harder. Early on I even had the audacity to promise God I would never indulge in pornography again. I tried hard to be stronger than my temptation, not knowing that the Bible teaches the opposite. Look at **2 Corinthians 12:9**

And He said to me, "My grace is sufficient for you, for My strength is made perfect in weakness." Therefore most gladly I will rather boast in my infirmities, that the power of Christ may rest upon me.

The Apostle Paul has just explained that he begged God to remove his thorn in the flesh. In this passage he doesn't explain what the thorn was, but this applies to you as well. For you, the thorn is a pornography addiction. This weakness of the flesh is actually a blessing, for it opens you to the power of God. As you take confidence in your weaknesses, it puts you into a position to have strength that can only come from God. We can only be confident in our weakness when we believe God's promise to become our strength.

This was the first step in emerging as an overcomer for me. The moment I fully understood that I could not beat this thing, I gave up my frail attempt at strength. Then I began learning how to rest in His strength.

Each time I share these things, someone says, "You are justifying sin. You are teaching that it's okay to live in sin."

Not so. I don't live in the sin that once bound me. I don't view pornography anymore. My addiction became a mere temptation, and over time, the temptation became so weak that it was a mere pebble under my shoe that I vaguely felt as I walked past. Saying that it's okay to be weak doesn't mean we are seeking to remain in weakness. It means we are giving up all attempts at self-effort so that we are strong in the Lord and the power of His might.[26]

Christ carries our infirmities and bears all our sorrows.[27] Since this is true, we should not be carrying a burden that God has placed upon Himself.

Never lose sight of God's love for you. Your greatest temptation won't be lust – it will be the temptation to disbelieve in God's love. The first time you fail, the enemy will whisper in your ear words of condemnation. He will tell you that God rejects you because of sin. This is a lie.

God has done you a great favor. All sin has been banished to the flesh, and your life has been born of the Spirit. Your new life in Christ is of the Spirit. This is why the Bible says that those who are born of God cannot sin. **1 John 3:9**

> Whoever has been born of God does not sin, for His seed remains in him; and he cannot sin, because he has been born of God.

One chapter earlier, John writes, "These things I write that you may not sin, but if anyone does sin, we have an advocate with the Father, Jesus Christ the righteous."

So how can John say that when we do sin, Jesus is our advocate, but then say that anyone born of God cannot sin? The book of Romans helps us to understand John's words more clearly. In Romans 7, the Apostle Paul begins to explain that the war going on in his mind is between the sin in his flesh, and the life he now has in the Spirit.

He then explains that when he looks to himself, though he has the will to do what is good and righteous, how to perform good he doesn't find. Instead, when he tries to be righteous by his own efforts, he ends up back in sin. Paul then explains, "In me, that is in my flesh, nothing good dwells."

Since this is true, anytime we are using human effort to try to overcome sin or do godly things, instead of producing good, we end

---

[26] Ephesians 6:10
[27] Isaiah 53:4

up back in sin. Even our good deeds are acts of pride, where the flesh is trying to make itself on par with God. When the flesh isn't boosting itself in pride, it retreats back into blatant sins. Look at the words of **Romans 7:17-18**

> ¹⁷ But now, *it is* no longer I who do it, but sin that dwells in me.
> ¹⁸ For I know that in me (that is, in my flesh) nothing good dwells; for to will is present with me, but *how* to perform what is good I do not find.

A few verses later, Paul laments, "O wretched man that I am, who will deliver me from this body of death," referring to the sin that draws him back into the old life of sin and death. How many times was this the cry of my heart? I tried to stop my lustful addictions, but how to stay in righteousness, I did not find in myself. Even when I tried to live godly, I ended up back into the sin that my will was trying to resist. Who could deliver me from my body of sin?

Thankfully I discovered what Paul said next. You also will discover this truth if you put your trust in God's deliverance instead of your own efforts. Look at the very next passage after Paul's lamentation of sin, **Romans 7:25**

> I thank God-- through Jesus Christ our Lord! So then, with the mind I myself serve the law of God, but with the flesh the law of sin.

When Paul was trying to become righteous for God, he found himself in sin instead of godliness. Yet, deliverance was already an accomplished fact. He was just looking in the wrong direction. When he looked to his flesh – which is where our human effort comes from, he found that he could do nothing but serve the law of sin. Sin is always in the flesh. Even when you are trying to do good, you are employing the body of sin, which is incapable of doing anything but serving the law of sin. The flesh will always seek gratification. The moment religious efforts stop gratifying the flesh, temptation blossoms with a fragrance we can't resist – unless we are not in the flesh.

The mind set on the Spirit is in life and peace.[28]

So let's compare what Romans is saying to what 1 John is saying. That which is born of God, our inner man, cannot sin. If our mind is in the Spirit, which is where our life in Christ always resides, then we will walk in victory. If we are viewing life through the flesh and trying to make our bodies obey a Christian standard that goes against everything the flesh craves, we will only find failure and frustration.

The inner man cannot sin. The flesh cannot do anything but sin. The heart of the problem is that we are conditioned to think through the flesh and make our identity in the flesh. Just think about the most popular recovery group's declaration, "Hello, my name is Eddie, and I am an addict."

What is the identity we are confessing? I am an addict. If your identity is an addict, you will be drawing from that identity. Some people find success in spite of this, but when we make our identity in the flesh, we will struggle to separate from our identity.

Romans 8:9 tells you, "You are not in the flesh, but in the Spirit if the Spirit of Christ dwells in you." Your identity has changed. The Bible calls our old nature 'the old man'. Our old man was crucified with Christ. Romans 6:6 says that our old man was crucified with Christ that the body of sin might be unemployed. Some translations say 'destroyed', but the Greek word from which this was translated means, to be rendered idle or unemployed.

Before Christ, your body ruled your mind. From an infant, your body hungered and you cried out for food. You felt discomfort, and you cried out to be changed. From birth, our entire lives are built around serving the body, but then we come to Christ and we are given a new nature, new spirit, and the body is rendered idle. It no longer sits at the command center of our lives.

But the body isn't dead. It still craves gratification and sin. So it uses any tactic in its power to take over your mind to call you back into its service. The Bible nails down your battle of addiction in **Romans 7:23**

---

[28] Romans 8:6

But I see another law in my members, warring against the law of my mind, and bringing me into captivity to the law of sin which is in my members.

In your flesh, sin reigns. If you are thinking according to the flesh, you will act according to the flesh, and temptation will be the urge of your body. If you are not in the flesh, your body will launch surprise attacks, trying to recapture your mind so you again serve it in its lusts.

Here we again see the great mercies of God. When you came to Christ, God gave you new life, which the Bible calls the inner man, new nature, spiritual man, and calls this new spirit 'you'. When your body is dead and buried, your spirit will continue on, and sin will not be present. The Apostle Peter called this new life an incorruptible seed, born again through the word of God, which lives and abides forever.

Understanding this is of vital importance. When you sin, you are harming your body, you are confining your spirit, you are robbing yourself of spiritual growth, and you're stepping outside of God's desire for your inheritance and blessing, but you are not corrupting your inner life of the Spirit.

The new spirit you have been given is in God. The Bible says we are hidden with God in Christ.[29] Sin cannot be in God's presence. The fact that you are the temple of the Holy Spirit[30] tells you that God has created a holy place to dwell within us. The Bible says that if we defile our bodies with sin, our flesh will be destroyed, but it does not say our spirits will be destroyed.

The Bible tells us that Jesus purchased eternal redemption for us.[31] Redemption is the payment for the debt we owe to the law for our sins. Our debt has been eternally paid, and we can never again be in debt to sin. All the consequences to sin are confined to our body. This can have severe consequences in this life, but cannot corrupt the life hidden in Christ.

---

[29] Colossians 3:3
[30] 1 Corinthians 3:16
[31] Hebrews 9:12

So our inner man cannot sin because it has been born of God. It is incorruptible because it is born of God and hidden in God through Christ. Sin abides in our body of flesh, and if we allow our minds to stay in the flesh, we will be in sin. This never changes. The battle-ground is here: are you living according to the inner man, or according to the body of sin? Are you setting your mind in the Spirit through faith in Christ, or are you putting your trust in the flesh?

We are trusting in the flesh by seeking both sin and self-righteousness. We serve the flesh when we believe temptation can supply our needs instead of God. We also serve the flesh when we believe the flesh can produce righteousness, instead of receiving the righteousness of God.

Most people never overcome, not because they don't try hard enough, but because they are employing the flesh to overcome itself. Because they are depending on human effort to succeed in order to become righteous, they are also depending on that same flesh not to turn against them to pursue lust. And when the flesh tires of resisting its cravings, control is lost.

Have you ever watched a lion tamer? The lion is never tamed. He is only constraining his natural desire, and the danger of attack never leaves. Even during a perfect performance, the lion continues to protest, though the crack of the whip creates enough fear to keep him in check.

Our flesh is like this beast, and fear is a terrible motivator. Unlike the lions, the flesh isn't caged a few minutes after each performance, so it's only a matter of time before the flesh rebels against your restrictions. Yet, the flesh is caged and confined through the Spirit. In the Spirit, we put the flesh out of the way, instead of employing it with the hope we can control it.

The Bible says that the just shall live by faith. Your life can only be lived in the Spirit by faith. When sin gets a temporary victory, do you grovel in the flesh in defeat, or do you turn your mind back to faith? Do you believe the promise that since God saved us when we were enemies, how much more will God continue to save us through Christ now that we are His children?[32]

---

[32] Romans 5:10

Your battle is not with pornography. It is not with sin. Your battle is to learn to start looking to Christ and learning to walk according to your new life, then the flesh has no power. Look at the words of **Ephesians 3:16-19**

> [16] that He would grant you, according to the riches of His glory, to be strengthened with might through His Spirit in the inner man,
> [17] that Christ may dwell in your hearts through faith; that you, being rooted and grounded in love,
> [18] may be able to comprehend with all the saints what *is* the width and length and depth and height--
> [19] to know the love of Christ which passes knowledge; that you may be filled with all the fullness of God.

Don't bother asking God to strengthen your flesh. Until the day when God redeems all things to Himself at the resurrection, your body will not be subject to the law of God. The Bible says that the flesh is not subject to the law of God and indeed it cannot be. For this reason, those who are in the flesh cannot please God.[33] When we receive strength in our inner man, the flesh is overcome – not strengthened.

If you are like me, you have wasted many prayers trying to get God to make your flesh act like a good Christian. Many nights I prayed for God to take the desire for sin away, take the addiction away, and help my flesh stop sinning. God never answered those prayers because they were based on my ignorance that the flesh cannot be subject to the law of God. It must be relegated back to where God sent it – to the unemployment line.

Review the above passage again. Where does strength come from? God gives us the might of the Spirit through the inner man. You have been empowered to defeat the flesh. You have the might of God. The Bible says that the same power that raised Jesus from the dead dwells in you, and will give life to your mortal bodies through the Spirit who dwells in you.[34]

---

[33] Romans 8:7-8
[34] Romans 8:11-14

When you live by the Spirit, the inner man, who is already empowered by God, will bring your flesh under its control. The body cannot control itself, but when we are living according to the life of faith, God's Spirit within us has the power to use the life of the Spirit to cause you to walk in newness of life. The flesh, once dethroned, is bound by the Spirit and we can now use the members of our bodies as instruments of righteousness.[35]

An important truth to understand is that you can't do this. You are putting your trust in the promise of God, and as you learn to walk by faith, the power of the Spirit renews your mind, and brings your body under control through His life.

It cannot work the other way around. Most people try to bring their flesh under control so God will be pleased, thinking that this will make them righteous. They are trying to reach the life of the Spirit through the body. This is impossible. We begin from the life of the Spirit, renew our minds through the word and the Spirit, and as our minds are centered on Christ, the body has no choice but return to its unemployed state.

Also take note of verse 19. The fullness of Christ within you passes knowledge, or goes beyond the ability to understand. Humanized Christianity has little power because people are limiting God to operate within their mind's ability to understand. Jesus compared the Kingdom of God to a farmer planting seeds. He scatters the seeds and rests. The seed springs up, though he doesn't know how this happens, but he watches it grow until it ripens, then he reaps the harvest.[36]

As you sow the word in your heart and begin living by faith, the life of Christ begins to emerge in your behavior, and you don't know how this works, but it does.

We rest and cultivate our spiritual life, believing that God will produce fruitfulness in our lives. How does taking my eyes off my sins and stop trying to change my behavior work, but investing my life into putting forth my best effort doesn't work? I don't know how. I just know that as I learn to walk in the love of God, the flesh

---

[35] Romans 6:13
[36] Matthew 4:26-29

dies, and new life emerges. Human reasoning says you must focus on yourself to improve yourself. God's word says to die to self, and focus on Christ. The promise is, those who try to save their life will lose it, but those who die to their life in this world will find new life.[37]

It is God's job to subdue your sins. It is God's job to produce the works of righteousness in you. Let's look at two passages that help clarify this. First look at **Micah 7:19**

> He will again have compassion on us, And will subdue our iniquities. You will cast all our sins Into the depths of the sea.

This Old Testament passage is pointing to the coming New Covenant, which we are now in. The Bible says that God hid His face for a moment through the law, but now we are in His everlasting kindness.[38] Here we are told that God forgave us and cast ALL our sins into the depths of the sea. The word 'all' is not referring to man's temporal concept.

We think that God is limited to our past sins, but all our sins were in the future when Jesus paid the debt. God is not bound by time, and when He performed the eternal work of redemption, He did not wait for us to sin, but took care of sin, once and for all time. Now we enter into His completed work through faith.

Equally important is the promise that God subdues our iniquities. It begins with His compassion on us. Because He loves and cares for you, and God knows that you are incapable of subduing your flesh, He has promised to subdue sin in your flesh. As you trust God, you are releasing your flesh to Him. It takes more trust to give God your sins than it does to try to do it yourself. It takes more trust to present your sins to God than it does to present your righteousness to Him.

Once you trust God, He takes the flesh and suppresses it. Where you lacked strength, God gave you the power of the Spirit through your inner man, and through the Spirit the lusts of the flesh

---

[37] Luke 17:33
[38] Isaiah 54:8

are crucified (or put to death)[39] so you can reign in righteousness.[40] Being human, when you drift back in the flesh and it again rises up with its lusts, you are called to again trust in the Spirit so you can walk in newness of life.

Spiritual maturity is not instant. When you begin to trust God, your tendency is to trust the flesh and waiver back to the old way of thinking. Think about temptation. Temptation promises that if you partake of this lust, you will be satisfied. It looks appealing and you feel a craving, so you go for it. When you emerge from temptation, do you feel satisfied? There is always an emptiness. Satisfaction becomes harder and harder to find, yet the lie looks so good, we believe it will work the next time.

As you begin discovering the satisfaction of the life of the Spirit, the temptations will grow weaker. The more you learn to walk in faith, the harder it will be for temptation to get a grip on your mind. God doesn't cast you out of His sight when you trust temptation. He says, "You were walking with Me above temptation. Why did you doubt?" Then He calls you to trust in Him, take His hand to be pulled from the miry clay of the flesh, and He raises you above temptation again to walk in the Spirit by faith.

When I was learning to recover from my addictions, I had times when it was hard to resist. Because I still believed sin nullified my acceptance of God, sometimes I stayed in temptation because I had no strength to climb out.

The day I truly understood that God's acceptance is based on Christ, and not myself, and everything was a gift of God's unearned favor, my life began to change. The next time I fell, I felt the condemnation of the devil, but I believed God instead. I immediately started walking in faith, knowing that I was accepted, and that His gift of righteousness was a gift and not something I earned. Then I found myself walking in the Spirit again. I still kicked myself, but I confessed my Advocate, and His promise over me. Condemnation dissipated and I began enjoying the satisfaction of fellowship. This led me to discover that walking with God through

---

[39] Romans 8:13
[40] Romans 5:17

every temptation and trial was more satisfying than anything of the old life.

The next time temptation came, I didn't feel the same internal response of my flesh. When I lost sight of faith and began to drift into the flesh, I fell again. Yet over time, the falls began to become farther apart. In the last few years, the temptation is hardly noticeable. The flesh has lost power in that area of my life, and I can honestly say, "My name is Eddie. I am NOT and addict." I don't even desire these things, for why would I give up the satisfaction I have in Christ for the empty shell of gratification in the flesh?

But wait, there's more! Not only has God promised to forgive our sins, bury them in the sea, and subdue our flesh's desire for iniquity, but God promised to create in us a heart for righteousness. Look at **Ezekiel 36:26-27**

> 26 "I will give you a new heart and put a new spirit within you; I will take the heart of stone out of your flesh and give you a heart of flesh.
> 27 "I will put My Spirit within you and cause you to walk in My statutes, and you will keep My judgments and do *them.*

This promise is yours! It is another Old Testament promise that we now have in the New Covenant of Christ. God takes away our old heart (which is our old nature), and gives us a new heart with a new spirit. This is the inner man. We have a new nature, which is what it means to be born again. Not only that, but God gives us His Spirit, and we now have perfect fellowship with God.

This is why the Bible calls us the temple of the Holy Spirit.[41] God has cleansed our inner being, made a place of perfection for Himself, and our inner man (spirit) has been perfected,[42] and dwells with God in our inner sanctuary. Now you have the invitation to walk in the Spirit, where your outer life can come in line with the inner life you have been given. The outward perfection of your behavior only emerges as you learn to walk according to the inner

---

[41] 1 Corinthians 3:16
[42] Hebrews 10:14

man. You are always in fellowship with God according to the inner man. Now you need to discover the reality of your inner life.

Not only that, but because our new spirit is in God and of God, it has the same desires as God. It is in our nature to do God's ways because our heart's desire is for righteousness.

You don't have to make yourself obey. As you learn to walk in that fellowship of God you have been given, you will naturally do the things that are in agreement with God. This is why we see in the New Testament that those who were never under the law and did not know the law of the Bible, did by nature the things written in the law, proving that God had written it on their hearts.[43]

You don't have to figure out this walk of faith. Through studying the word with the understanding that all things point us to the cross, where everything is a free gift of the Spirit, you will learn to walk by faith. It will be your desire to walk in righteousness. You don't have to say, "I must do," you will have the craving to do the things that are pleasing to God.

Your new nature wants the things of God. As you renew your mind in the word, the Holy Spirit will enlighten your understanding, and the revelation of your inner man will become part of your life. You will grow in understanding, and the more you seek the treasures of the Spirit, the more you will find. Each discovery you receive by faith displaces more and more of the flesh.

The Christian life is all about learning to walk by faith. The Bible says that God has given you all things that pertain to life and godliness, and we receive these because we are a partaker of God's divine nature. Look at **2 Peter 1:3-4**

> [3] As His divine power has given to us all things that *pertain* to life and godliness, through the knowledge of Him who called us by glory and virtue,
> [4] by which have been given to us exceedingly great and precious promises, that through these you may be partakers of the divine nature, having escaped the corruption *that is* in the world through lust.

---

[43] Romans 2:14-15

You escape the lust of the world one way – by becoming a partaker of God's nature. His power has given you everything you need to live in godliness, and to experience life. But until you believe God, these promises remain unrealized. They are received by faith.

Let's end this chapter with one other passage. Look at **2 Corinthians 5:21**

> For He made Him who knew no sin *to be* sin for us, that we might become the righteousness of God in Him.

You are righteous in God's eyes for one reason – you are in Christ and have received the gift of righteousness. You stay righteous the same way you entered it – by faith in Christ. The Bible says that Abraham believed God, and God credited Abraham with God's own righteousness.[44] Scripture explains that this wasn't only for Abraham, but it is also for you and I.

When you feel defeated, confess your promise of victory. When you feel sinful, confess this truth, "I am the righteousness of God in Christ."

When your flesh rises up and seems to be overcoming you, confess this truth, "Lord you promised that You have given me Your Spirit, and promised that the same power that raised Jesus from the dead is in me, and will give life to my physical body. I confess and trust in Your power over my temptations."[45]

When you had a momentary defeat, confess the words of Ephesians 1:6, "I am accepted in the beloved – Christ. I am accepted by God through Christ for the glory of God's grace."

The more you stay in the promises of God, the less you will stay in defeat. The more you walk by faith, the more you'll learn to stay in the life of the Spirit.

Remember the words of scripture, "This is the victory that overcomes the world, our faith."[46] You already have the power of God's Spirit. He has already made you an overcomer. You are

---

[44] Galatians 3:6-9
[45] Romans 8:11
[46] 1 John 5:4

already more than a conqueror. Learn to receive these promises and walk by faith. Believe God over your addiction. Believe God over your failures and struggles. Believe God – even when you have failed.

The success of Christ is not dependent upon you. Your success is dependent upon Christ. Christ's righteousness is not overthrown because of your sin. Your sin is overthrown by the righteousness of Christ – which has been freely given to you. You didn't become righteous because of what you did, nor do you lose God's righteousness because of what you have done.

Walk by faith in His righteousness, and the flesh has no power to overthrow you. The flesh that now haunts you will be under your feet by the power of the Spirit of Christ who dwells in you!

Discussion Questions

1. Explain what it means when God says, "My grace is sufficient, for My strength is made perfect in your weakness."

2. Why does the Bible say that when we sin, we should have confidence in our Advocate, Jesus Christ, but then says that the person born of God cannot sin?

3. Review Romans 7:17-18 and 1 John 3:9. Where does sin dwell?
4. Where do we find righteousness?

5. Read Ephesians 4:22-24, 1 Corinthians 2:13-16, and Romans 8:5-10. The natural mind (carnal) cannot understand or subject itself to the spiritual life of Christ. So what happens if we are looking to ourselves for the ability to live godly?

6. How do you put off your former conduct (the old man)? Reread these three passages for more clarity.

7. Read Hebrews 11:6. How does living by faith apply to our previous questions?

8. Review Romans 7:25. In the flesh (human effort) are you serving God or sin? What if you are trying to act godly?

9. Review Ephesians 3:16-19. Where does strength come from?

10. How is the Christian strengthened, in our mind, outward behavior, or in our spirit?

11. Is the inner man limited to human knowledge, or ability to figure out how the Spirit works? Explain.

12. Review Ezekiel 36:26-27. Can someone have true godliness without having a new spirit?

13. If we have the promise that God will be the catalyst for walking in obedience, why do so many people struggle with sin?

14. Review 2 Peter 1:3-4. What does it mean to be a partaker of God's nature?

15. How does this apply to your struggle to overcome addiction?

16. Read Galatians 3:6-9. How are you made righteous?

17. Read Galatians 3:15-17. If a man's covenant can't be annulled, what does this tell us about a covenant confirmed by God in Christ?

18. Can your sin annul God's covenant of promise - which includes the gift of righteousness?

19. How does understanding the certainty of God's promise help you to overcome the old life of the flesh?

If you found this book helpful, please take a moment to rate it on Amazon.com

Learning to Walk in the Spirit

Why did the Old Testament say that it is better to be in the house of mourning than the house of joy,[47] but when Jesus delivered the New Covenant to His disciples, He said, "I write these things that your joy may be full?"

In the Old Testament, their sacrifices and confessions could never take away sin. The annual animal sacrifice was a yearly reminder of the wages of sin that they were under, and the animal stood in their place as a temporary sacrifice.[48] They could never rejoice that their sins were gone, so the house of mourning was an acknowledgment of their guilt and sorrow over sin.

Our sins have been fully removed in Christ. The New Testament was sealed by Christ's blood, who took away the sin of the world.[49] The Old Testament worshipper had to focus on their sins and the hope of God's mercy. The New Testament worshipper has the joy of God's revealed mercy, and His declaration that Christ became our sin so that we are now the righteousness of God in Christ.[50]

The people of the Old Testament were of the flesh, still bound to sin. We are a people who died to the flesh and were born of the Spirit, set free from sin.[51]

Now our focus is to learn how to walk according to our new life, as we learn to leave the flesh behind. Instead of reflecting on the sins of the past, we are discovering the depth of what we have in the Spirit. Instead of living under the burden of condemnation, we are living under the promise. God has taken away the barrier of sin between us and Him, and all He has is now freely given to us. Jesus called it the abundant life for a reason.[52]

---

[47] Ecclesiastes 7:4
[48] Hebrews 10:1-4
[49] John 1:29
[50] 2 Corinthians 5:21
[51] Romans 6:7
[52] John 10:10

Walking by faith is walking in the Spirit, but learning how to live in the Spirit is a great mystery to many people. Very few churches teach on this because few understand the grace-filled Christian life. If we teach grace without understanding the life of the Spirit, grace is then limited to human understanding.

The fleshly minded legalist calls this a license to sin because they have no concept of the power of the Spirit. They are ruled by the flesh through the law. In the same way, the fleshly minded progressive/liberal Christian lives outside of the power of the Spirit, and is ruled by the flesh without the law.

Both legalism and progressivism are two ends of the same spectrum. The flesh is still the flesh, whether we serve the flesh through harsh religious living, or permissive religious living, or nonreligious living. We don't escape the flesh through the law, nor do we escape the flesh by casting off traditionalism. We escape the flesh through the Spirit, and as we learn to receive of God through the spirit, the flesh becomes irrelevant, regardless of what mask it hides behind.

Now is the time to reverse your thinking. You have probably heard that if you can stop sinning, God will receive you, or you will be able to live a holy life. Wrong! You must enter into God's holiness in order to stop sinning. You enter the promise so that you are a receiver of the power of grace. Consider the words of **Galatians 5:16**

> I say then: Walk in the Spirit, and you shall not fulfill the lust of the flesh.

Notice, this does not say to stop lusting so you can walk in the Spirit. It promises you that as you learn to walk in the Spirit, the flesh no longer has the power to fulfill its desire for lust. And don't forget that lust is not only sensuality; it is also anger, jealousy, greed, selfishness, and any other thing the flesh desires. The word 'lust' means 'intense desire'. The desire to avenge a wrong is just as much the lust of the flesh as a pornography addiction. So is greed. So is everything the flesh uses to gratify itself.

The reason your efforts to break your addiction haven't worked is because you have been duped. The church has been duped. Duped people are teaching a duped doctrine – that if you stop sinning, you will find righteousness. The opposite is true. When you learn to receive the promise of righteousness (which is already yours), you will stop sinning. Righteousness drives out sin.

The biggest problem of Christianized religion is that most people cannot separate the Old Testament from the New Covenant. Under the old, the people had to bring their flesh under control, or be guilty of breaking God's law. As we can see in the teaching of the New Testament, the flesh cannot cease from sin, and the law was given to reveal to man how sinful he is, so he stops looking to himself to find righteousness.[53]

The Bible says that the law was given so sin might appear to be sin, and that sin, through the commandment, might become exceedingly sinful. The reason is that we were born as flesh (carnal), but the law is spiritual and incompatible with our flesh.[54] So the commandments of the law are not intended to make man righteous, but to reveal to man how sinful he really is.

As an addict, you have a great blessing before you. So do I. At the height of my addiction, I fully understood that I could not make myself pure. I knew I was exceedingly sinful, and that in me, I could not find good. For this reason, it was easy to recognize that unless God rescued me, I was hopeless. This is an understanding that the average church member has difficulty grasping. If the church attender is succeeding in keeping a dumbed down version of the law, they evaluate themselves as good, even though the law declares them as guilty.

You and I had an unacceptable flaw that made it impossible to fit into the church mindset. No one keeps the law, but man has always dumbed down the law to make himself feel like an achiever. This is why Jesus confronted religious people with the full measure of the law. "You say you have never committed adultery, but I say to you that even if you look at a woman to lust after her, you have

---

[53] Romans 3:19-21
[54] Romans 7:13-14

committed adultery in your heart."[55] Religion hated Jesus because Jesus called the dumbed down version of the law an act of sin. And it still is so today.

But those who learn to leave the flesh and the law that condemns the flesh behind, have died to what they were once held by.[56] Jesus said, "If anyone desires to come after Me, let him deny himself, take up his cross and follow Me."[57]

Denying yourself does not mean to merely resist temptation. It means to deny yourself self-glorification. It is to deny that righteousness comes from yourself. It is to deny your personal religion, self-reliance, and all personal efforts to please God.

The cross is the death of the flesh, so to take up the cross is to enter the life of faith, where the Spirit crucifies the flesh, and you follow Christ into the fullness of the life of the Spirit. The cross is not something you do for God. No one nails himself to the cross. He submits to those who nail him to the cross. Jesus laid down His life and allowed the Roman soldiers to nail him to the cross. Now we, by faith, allow the Spirit to nail our old life to the cross so we are freed from the flesh so we can now follow Christ.

Follow Christ, not do for Christ. There is only one work you can do for God, and it is found in **John 6:28-29**

> [28] Then they said to Him, "What shall we do, that we may work the works of God?"
>
> [29] Jesus answered and said to them, "This is the work of God, that you believe in Him whom He sent."

The only thing you can do for God is to believe in the finished work of God, which is the cross of Jesus Christ. The only human act in the Christian life is to believe what God has revealed through Christ. Faith is given to us by God.[58] Faith is when God reveals His promise or intent to you, gives you the power to believe, and invites you to enter into His work. When this occurs, your only work

---

[55] Matthew 5:27-28
[56] Romans 7:6
[57] Matthew 16:24
[58] Romans 12:3, Galatians 5:22, 1 Corinthians 12:9

is to let go of your will and personal efforts, or to reject the revelation of faith and attempt to do the work on your own – which is impossible.

Religion teaches you to do your work for God. Faith calls you to enter into God's finished work by the invitation of the Spirit.

You have already been delivered. God's work for you is already complete. The only thing not complete is you learning how to respond to His work by faith. As we explore these truths of scripture, you will likely feel the drawing of the Spirit as God invites you to enter into His finished work of deliverance.

You don't become addiction-free for God. You are invited into faith, where your addiction has already been defeated. Addiction is of the flesh, and it cannot enter the life of the Spirit. As you learn to stop looking to the flesh and begin looking to the Spirit, the power of the flesh loses its grip and falls away. Sin cannot go where you are going.

The flesh cannot defeat the Spirit. It can only bluff you into believing it has a claim over you. Jesus came to set the captives free, give sight to the blind, and heal the broken-hearted.[59] Until now, you were blind to the revelation of grace. Jesus is grace, for the Bible says that He is full of grace and truth.[60] The Bible also says that the law was sent through Moses, but grace *came* through Jesus Christ.[61] The impersonal law was a letter of condemnation sent, but the love of God came through grace in the person of Jesus Christ.

He set the captives free, which means your freedom has already been purchased. He heals the broken-hearted, which means your fractured and incomplete heart has been healed, and that your new heart is waiting for you to receive it. Sin only comes through a broken heart, for a healthy heart is complete, and needs no fleshly substitutes to fill in the gaps, which create our need. Take careful note of this amazing passage in **Titus 2:11-14**

---

[59] Luke 4:18-19
[60] John 1:14
[61] John 1:17

> [11] For the grace of God that brings salvation has appeared to all men,
> [12] teaching us that, denying ungodliness and worldly lusts, we should live soberly, righteously, and godly in the present age,
> [13] looking for the blessed hope and glorious appearing of our great God and Savior Jesus Christ,
> [14] who gave Himself for us, that He might redeem us from every lawless deed and purify for Himself *His* own special people, zealous for good works.

Jesus, the person of grace, came to bring salvation. That is your salvation from sin. Those who are established in grace (which is Christ and all He has provided) naturally cease from sin. For grace teaches us to deny ungodliness and worldly lusts. Grace teaches us how to live in godliness, righteousness, and soberness. A sober mind is not controlled by the flesh, addictions, or temptation. It is clearly focused and established in the purity of the Spirit. Grace teaches us to focus on our hope in Christ, knowing that we have been given all things that pertain to life and godliness.[62]

Grace teaches you that Jesus has redeemed you from every lawless deed. The Bible says that Jesus purchased our eternal redemption when He applied His own blood to the altar in heaven, once and for all.[63] Eternal redemption means that not only has your past debt to sin been paid, but the payment is eternally applied. Your future sins have already been paid, and you can never again be indebted to sin.

The above passage also tells you that grace has already purified you and made you into a special person, reserved for Christ. You are already purified, now you need to learn to walk in the purity of faith.

Finally, grace creates a people zealous for good works. As you learn to walk in grace, not only will sin fall away, and not only will purity and godliness emerge, but the desire of your heart will

---

[62] 2 Peter 1:3
[63] Hebrews 9:12

blossom into a desire for good works. Today your addiction may be the desire ruling your heart, but as you learn to walk by faith in God's grace, that sinful desire will die, and a new desire will emerge. Your new desire will be a fulfilling life that has meaning and purpose. You will naturally be drawn to do what God has gifted you to do, and because your works are in God, it is rewarding, fulfilling, and has eternal significance.

You can forget about pornography. It will become a distant memory, and instead of having a compulsion that you hate, you will soon have a desire that you love. No more guilt. No more fear. No more regret. You will have a desire that pleases you and God, and your heart will be at rest and in peace.

Now here is the most difficult part of this book. No one can say, "Follow these steps and you'll be walking in the Spirit." Walking in the Spirit is the life of faith – trusting fully in Christ. Spiritual growth takes time. No infant is born into adulthood. Some children grow faster than others, and some minds mature faster than others.

Regardless of how long you have been a Christian, you need to begin the road to maturity. Sometimes you'll have a growth spurt, and other times things will be slow and steady. Sometimes you'll have setbacks, but those setbacks will become fewer as your growth becomes steadier.

The Bible tells us to sincerely desire the milk of the word, but as you grow out of milk, you'll begin to get into the meat of the word. Start spending time in the word, especially the epistles (or letters) of Paul.

I recommend starting with books in this order: Romans, Colossians, Galatians, Ephesians, Titus, 1 Timothy, 2 Timothy, 1 John, 1 Peter, 2 Peter, 1 Corinthians, 2 Corinthians.

Once you've spent time reading, rereading, and studying, begin to explore the rest of the scripture. These books will help lay a strong foundation, and help you understand the gospel of grace. Consider the words of **Romans 12:2**

> And do not be conformed to this world, but be transformed by the renewing of your mind, that you may prove what *is* that good and acceptable and perfect will of God.

Six times in the New Testament, we are told to renew our minds. If you do not renew daily, temptation will become stronger. The Bible tells us that the flesh is weak. Since this is true, if we allow our minds to drift back into the flesh, our weakness becomes our only strength, and a fall is inevitable. The temptations of the flesh only appear strong when our spiritual life becomes weak through neglect.

Don't study the Bible as a task to accomplish. Seek Christ through the word. You are seeking to discover the depths of the life of the Spirit. Pray for the Spirit to reveal His ways to you. Discover the treasures hidden for you to find. Memorize meaningful scriptures, but always study the context surrounding the passage you are memorizing.

Spend time in prayer – not only praying for specific needs, but learn to converse with God. You'll be amazed at how many times God opens your understanding to new insights during times of prayer.

Just as important, let me reiterate this one thing again. If you fall back into your addiction, do not fear. Do not receive condemnation. Believe and obey this passage from **Hebrews 4:16**

> Let us therefore come boldly to the throne of grace, that we may obtain mercy and find grace to help in time of need.

You are always welcomed by God. The time of need is when you have blown it. The throne of grace means the throne of God's favor. When you trust in God's favor, you will not only walk in the life of redemption, but you will find additional favor, which is God's gifts of love that helps you during your time of need. You receive mercy, which is not receiving punishment for sin, and you also receive grace, which is God's power and gifts of the Spirit. It is not based on your worthiness, but God's own nature of love.

The false gospel of condemnation says, "Get your life right and then you can come before God," but as you can see, God has commanded you to come before Him with confidence when you are in need, which is when you have sinned and blown it.

Never believe the lie that your weakness and failure takes you out of God's favor. Never believe the lie that you have to get your life right for God. Believe the truth that God favors you – even in your worst state, and it is His power that overcomes your weakness.

Learn to walk by faith, always turning your heart toward Christ. As you learn to walk in grace by faith, the flesh becomes powerless, and you'll discover the power of God to overcome any weakness, and the grace to defeat any sin. Love covers a multitude of sins.[64] Since God is love,[65] if you are in the love of God, your sins are more than covered.

The Bible tells us to know and believe in the love God has for us, and anyone who abides in God's love, abides in God.[66] In other words, to walk in the Spirit, you have to only believe in God's love, and abide in His love. Rest in the love of God and let His love do God's perfect work in you.

Never lose sight of this important truth – that you are God's treasure. When a prospector finds treasure, he mines it out of what is worthless, polishes it up, and makes it valuable. In our case, God has placed the treasure of new life within our body of flesh, and He has invited you and me to be a part of exposing the treasure. God wants you to delight in His work in your life, and He invites you to be a part of it so you can see your value emerging.

Sin is not your problem. Unbelief is your problem. Those who don't believe that God's love and acceptance is already a part of their lives will live in guilt and condemnation. Those who don't believe in grace will seek fulfillment in the flesh. The more you believe in what God has declared over you and what He is doing in

---

[64] 1 Peter 4:8
[65] 1 John 4:8, 1 John 4:16
[66] 1 John 4:16

you, the more you will allow the life of the Spirit to emerge. The moment you disbelieve, you are in the flesh.

If you disbelieve the promise that you are the righteousness of God in Christ, you will begin to put your trust in condemnation and sin. The moment you disbelieve that God has given you all things that pertain to both life and godliness, you will begin to trust in human efforts and the empty promises of the world.

When you disbelieve in the finished work of Christ that supplies all your needs, you will begin to trust in personal religion – including self-condemnation and perpetual repentance. False repentance is the person who fails and believes they must get their life right with God. True repentance is to take our minds out of the flesh, and rest our confidence in the promise of the Spirit. The word 'repent / repentance' is the Greek word 'metanoia', which means, to change the mind.

Biblical repentance is not groveling in guilt and the defeat of sin, trying to do some time of penance for God. Biblical repentance is to recognize our mind has slipped into a fleshly way of thinking, and we put our mind back in the Spirit – living by faith and focused on the love of God through Christ.

Lastly, keep this final thought in mind. The Bible says that as we look to the glory of Christ, we are transformed into that same image by the Spirit of God.[67] If you keep your focus on Christ, the grace given to you, the finished work of the cross, and the confident expectation of good because of His promises to you, the transformation of your life is both a guarantee, and the natural fruit of living in the Spirit. Trust and rest. Watch the transforming power of God do His work in your life!

Now begin your journey of faith, blessed by the love of God, and becoming a man built on the solid rock of Christ. Your success is already established by God. Believe and walk in it!

---

[67] 2 Corinthians 3:18

Discussion Questions

1. Read Hebrews 9:12 and 9:24-26, Hebrews 7:27, and Hebrews 10:10. How many times does Jesus have to deal with our sin?

2. The word redemption means to pay the debt we have to the law. In Hebrews 9:12, how long does Jesus' redemption last?

3. Can our temporary weakness defeat the eternal redemption of Christ?

4. Read Romans 8:3-4. How is the law fulfilled in us?

5. If man's weakness was why the law could not work, does man's weakness also limit the work of Christ?

6. If your failure could put you back under sin's power, would the new work of Christ be any better than the old work of the law?

7. What does it mean to renew your mind?

8. Can you grow into a mature Christian without spending time with God?

9. Read Proverbs 2:1-16. What does God's gift of wisdom protect you from?

10. How do you discover wisdom, knowledge, and understanding?

11. What does it mean that God stores up wisdom? How do you get what God has stored for you to find?

12. What does It mean to repent?

13. Has this book changed your perspective? If so, how?

14. Commit to reviewing the principles of this book until you grow in grace and see addiction begin to fade from your life.

A Word for the Wives

If you are a spouse of someone with a pornography addiction, there are some important truths for you to understand. The first thing you need to know is that you are not the cause of the problem, but you are an important part of the solution. Most women look at their husband's addiction as an attempt to make up what they lack. This is not true.

There is a reason why these movies and magazines change women in every issue. The fact is that any addiction of the flesh requires constant new stimulation. Because this is not based on true intimacy, it is 100% dependent on new experiences. What gave pleasure yesterday draws a lesser response today.

If you were a supermodel, it wouldn't change anything. The flesh is quickly desensitized, and like a drug, it needs more in order to get the same fulfillment. There comes a time when the addiction stops creating pleasure, and it becomes an attempt to feel normal – or to at least stop the withdrawals.

The biggest challenge a wife will face is the temptation of bitterness. I know a man who hasn't been in pornography for more than a decade, but his wife still disbelieves in him, and because her anger has turned into bitterness, there is little if any emotional connection between them. He had to learn to depend on the Lord, knowing his wife disconnected long ago.

When a woman refuses to accept the changes God is doing in her husband, it makes recovery a solo mission, and much more difficult. It's okay to not accept pornography in the relationship, but be an encourager instead of a condemner. The fact that he is trying to break free tells you he doesn't want the addiction. Consider the words of **Ecclesiastes 4:9-10**

> 9 Two *are* better than one, Because they have a good reward for their labor.
>
> 10 For if they fall, one will lift up his companion. But woe to him *who is* alone when he falls, For *he has* no one to help him up.

It is likely that your husband will fall many times on his road to freedom. Instead of getting angry, be an accountability partner.

If someone had cancer and fought to beat it, they would have some good days and some bad days. If it were cancer, would you lash out at him on a bad day? When he felt defeated, would you scold him? No, you would encourage him to press on and you'd become a partner in strength.

Pornography addiction is a cancer of the soul. It is very curable, but for most people it is a hard recovery. When he has a bad day, he'll be down on himself. He is not glad he fell – he is probably very discouraged.

When I struggled to overcome, no one had my back. The church wasn't there. No one I knew at the time had this struggle – or at least didn't admit it. I never fell and enjoyed it. I would always be kicking myself, down on myself, and discouraged. How I would have benefited from a book like this, telling me this was a normal setback on the road to recovery, and to keep pressing on. I wish someone had explained this to my wife, who felt betrayed by the addiction, and still has a hard time not viewing me as the man I was instead of the man the Lord is shaping me into. Old emotional scars have a hard time healing.

Your temptation will be to harbor your feelings of pain. The hurt will try to become anger, and the anger will solidify into bitterness – if you allow it to do so. Your temptation will be to point at his failures and say, "See, you haven't changed." You'll be tempted to view him through the eyes of bitterness. This also is normal, but you are called to the extraordinary.

The normal life of the flesh holds on to wrongs, but the new life of the Spirit holds on to hope. If you establish yourself in the love of God, you'll experience the promise that love (God's gift of agape love to us) keeps no record of wrong.[68] Abiding in God's love makes it impossible to allow bitterness to sap you of a thriving life God intends for both of you. A heart of bitterness departs from the

---

[68] 1 Corinthians 13:4-8

Lord, making it impossible to experience God's best for you and your husband.[69]

The same truths that lead your husband into recovery also lead you into the satisfied life of the Spirit. If you are dependent upon your husband in order to find fulfillment, you both are being set up for failure. The woman who is satisfied in the Lord will also be satisfied in her husband. Then when both of you are drawing closer to Christ, you will naturally grow closer to each other.

Don't look at your husband first; look at Christ. Let's look at the promise and warning of **Jeremiah 17:5-8**

> [5] Thus says the LORD: "Cursed *is* the man who trusts in man And makes flesh his strength, Whose heart departs from the LORD.
> [6] For he shall be like a shrub in the desert, And shall not see when good comes, But shall inhabit the parched places in the wilderness, *In* a salt land *which is* not inhabited.
> [7] "Blessed *is* the man who trusts in the LORD, And whose hope is the LORD.
> [8] For he shall be like a tree planted by the waters, Which spreads out its roots by the river, And will not fear when heat comes; But its leaf will be green, And will not be anxious in the year of drought, Nor will cease from yielding fruit.

Of course, the word 'man' is mankind in the general sense. It applies to both male and female. The one who is dependent upon a man (or another person) is setting themselves up for failure. That person will become dry in their soul, bitter, and will not even see when good comes.

Human nature proves this regularly. When two people first fall in love, they become feeling dependent, but when the feelings fade, they become takers. Over time, we fall into the warning of this scripture that we will not see when good comes. The person we are depending on for happiness stops making us happy, and then we become blind to the dozens of things right, and focus only

---

[69] Hebrews 12:15

on what bothers us. Then instead of seeing good, we only see the bad, the hurt, and the failures. As this person becomes more unfulfilled, bitterness grows, and eventually it can become hatred.

But the one who looks to the Lord has a watered life that will flourish, even when the times of drought hit our lives. Our soul will remain vibrant and fruitful, even if others let us down.

The truth is that when someone emerges from an addiction, that life will flourish more than it would have without the addiction, for that person has learned to receive the life of the Spirit. Your marriage can be stronger than before, and even stronger than it would have had your spouse never fallen into this addiction.

God never merely restores. He restores abundantly above what the enemy has taken. Don't be a spouse trapped in the barrenness of bitterness while the recovered addict is abounding with new life. It's the Lord's desire for you both to flourish together, and have the testimony of God resting upon you and your marriage.

The enemy will come to you and stir up old feelings of bitterness. Yet if you release those into God's care through forgiveness, they will have no power over you. And don't believe the lie that we forgive but don't forget. True forgiveness is founded upon God's gift of agape love, which thinks no evil, but believes in hope, while keeping no record of wrong.

The life-giving forgiveness that God calls you into also calls us to refuse to allow our minds to revisit wrongs. The Bible promises that the person who is resting in faith will take every thought captive, and submit them to the obedience of Christ.[70] His obedience has overcome all sin, and by faith you enter – and release your spouse – into the accomplished obedience of Christ, which is credited to both of you. But only if you obey the call of faith.

Unforgiveness is our heart's declaration that we don't believe God, and must become the judge over the sins of others. It is to say, "God won't handle this rightly, so I must take up my own cause." But there is not one example where unforgiveness or

---

[70] 2 Corinthians 10:5

bitterness has made anyone's life better. It ALWAYS poisons the heart of its possessor.

Just as God rights every wrong in your husband's life, God will right every wrong done to you. Everything the addiction has robbed will be abundantly over restored, if you abide in the love of God by faith. Long-term anger and bitterness is caused by distrusting God, and trusting in the flesh. Anger is of the flesh. Bitterness is of the flesh. Even hurt is of the flesh. The life of promise replaces the hurt with grace, joy, and restoration.

I've seen many women who refused to let go of their hurt, and eagerly sacrificed peace and the promise of God with bitterness. If we are walking according to the flesh, it's hard to not treasure bitterness. Even though we can see the evidence of its damage, people still cling to bitterness.

If you view your husband through the eyes of bitterness, you'll see things that cause more bitterness. If you see your husband through the filter of distrust, you'll see distrust. If you view him through the eyes of your anger, you'll interpret his actions as an assault against anger. You'll see intent in him that isn't there. Some of these things may have been present before his life began changing, but your feelings are constantly reviving in your heart what God has put in the grave.

It's also important to understand that you can't see outwardly what God is doing inwardly. Sometimes it takes time to see the fruitful life of the Spirit emerging in outward behavior. It's also easier to notice mistakes than it is to notice when mistakes don't occur.

You will feel justified in anger and bitterness. These feelings may indeed be just, but do you want to live under a system of justice, or a system of grace? We can't demand justice without submitting ourselves to that same system. But if you live for grace, you'll be amazed at what flourishes in the garden of your life.

I've witnessed many hurt spouses digging up the grave their husband is escaping from, and flinging its buried bones into the present. When we are hurt, it's hard to accept God's mercy in the life of those who hurt us. It's even harder to accept God's grace (abundant favor) toward those who hurt us. But all wrongs, sins, and failures are in the flesh. As he steps into the life of the Spirit, those wrongs are dead. As you step into the life of the Spirit, the wrongs against you are dead. And the wrongs you have done are also dead.

You cannot take wrongs into the life of the Spirit. You can't take bitterness into the life of the Spirit. Or anger. Or sin. Or anything else of the flesh. While you hold on to pain and bitterness, you are not allowing God to draw you into the life of the Spirit.

God's change in your husband's life is for you, also. A marriage walking together in the Spirit is a treasure this world rarely sees. His addiction will become a blessing for you and him, if you place your complete confidence in God. Then you can walk on this journey of discovery together.

The sad reality is that addiction divides a marriage in one of two ways. Either the addict believes he is forever bound to sin and he lives for the flesh, but his wife learns to depend on God. She grows in the Spirit while he flounders in the flesh. Or the man discovers that the life of the Spirit is his escape from addiction. He begins following Christ, but his frustrated wife refuses to come.

How sweet it is when both the husband and the wife recognize that the flesh is worthless, and gladly release their version of the flesh into God's hands. Then they will both walk together on the journey of the discovery of grace, which breaks every chain and heals every wounded heart.[71]

Pray together. Seek the Lord together. Forgive each other. Refuse to justify your own acts of the flesh, but roll those cares onto God's shoulders, and walk by faith. If someone must measure up to a standard to make you happy, you aren't walking by faith. If you are looking at Christ and making Him your confidence, the failures of the other become God's responsibility, and you are free to love them without condition. Roll all your cares onto God's shoulders where they belong.[72] Roll your struggles onto the Lord, and your hurts onto the Lord.

---

[71] Luke 4:18
[72] 1 Peter 5:6-7

Let your heart hurt for your spouse because you long to see them out of their bondage, but don't allow your flesh to demand you hurt for yourself. This is only natural, but we are called above the natural state of the flesh. Roll your care of the other person onto God with prayer for their escape, and roll the care of your own needs onto God's shoulders with confidence that what you lack, God has already supplied.

The greater tragedy is to be hurt, and to refuse God's supply. To wallow in self-grief is a cheap substitute for resting in the arms of the Lord, and allowing Him to carry your sorrows. When you trade sorrow for blessing, bitterness for joy, and anger for peace, you'll find what true happiness is all about. And I'm confident that God will restore your relationship as He invites both of you into the life of victory.

Appendix A

John 3:3
> Jesus answered and said to him, "Most assuredly, I say to you, unless one is born again, he cannot see the kingdom of God."

We have been given a completely new life in Christ. One does not merely convert to Christianity. We are born from above. This is the difference between new life and religion. Religion promises freedom, but it oppresses.

According to the Bible, the law was given to reveal to every person that they are guilty and cannot be righteous by human effort.[73] Yet this revelation is not to condemn us, but to point us to new life. The message of condemnation is written to show religious people that religion cannot save. Religion is man trying to elevate himself to God in some way.

Some religions teach that man obtains divinity, or works to become a god. Others teach that man must act within certain boundaries in order to become accepted by God. Even Christianity, if it stoops down to merely creating boundaries, becomes another form of bondage through religion. Both sin and religion oppress. But Jesus said that He came to set the captives free, and to give us abundant life.

Don't allow your idea of Christianity to be skewed by well-meaning, but confused messages of what God demands. God demands only one thing of you – faith. Faith is believing what God reveals to you by promise. It's the call to trust in Christ alone.

Our example of the life of faith is Abraham, who believed God's promise, and God credited Abraham with God's own righteousness. And you have more than what was available to Abraham.

---

[73] Romans 3:19-20

Through Christ, we have been given the life that Abraham and the Old Testament saints hoped for. The Bible promised those in the Old Testament that the day would come when God would take away their heart hardened by sin, give them a new spirit, and He would place His Spirit within us, who would teach us how to walk in God's ways – and that without even having to worry about rules. Our nature will change, so our desires will change also. Look at this promise in **2 Corinthians 5:17**

> Therefore, if anyone *is* in Christ, *he is* a new creation; old things have passed away; behold, all things have become new.

When you receive Christ, you are not committing your life to God and promising to do religious things. You are surrendering your old sinful nature to God, and He takes it away, and replaces it with a new nature, which is born through the Holy Spirit. God forgives your sins, removes the nature that was born into sin, and gives you a new nature that is born from God.

The Bible calls this 'being crucified with Christ'. When Jesus died on the cross, He died as a sinner in your place, and He exchanges His sinless life for your sinful life. It's the great exchange. The Bible explains this in **2 Corinthians 5:21**

> For He [God] made Him [Jesus] who knew no sin *to be* sin for us, that we might become the righteousness of God in Him.

You don't do religious acts to become righteous. You believe this promise – that Jesus became your sin, and when you put your trust in Him, you become His righteousness. Then you are righteous because you have been credited with God's own righteousness.

This is why the Bible says that without faith, it is impossible to please God. Faith is when God reveals His gift of love to you, which is grace, and you believe in His love. Then when you put your trust in Him, you are credited as being the righteousness of God, just as Abraham was.

Let me share another passage that helps us to understand this. If you are not familiar with Abraham, he was the Old

Testament man God called out of the world. He became the carrier of the promise, and was the forefather of the Jewish people, who became the nation of Israel.

Abraham lived by faith. God gave Abraham the promises of God, and even when he sinned and made mistakes, God dealt with him according to his faith in the promise, not according to his own works. Abraham was before the law was given. The law was conditional upon man doing his part first, with the conditional promise that if people do all the law commanded and did not do anything the law forbid, then he could be under the promise. But if man failed on any point, then he was under the curse of the law.[74] And everyone failed because their human nature cannot be perfect.

When God gave the law, it was conditional upon man's ability to be perfect – which was impossible. And the purpose of the law was to show mankind that it was impossible. That's why the Bible calls the law our tutor, which brings us to Christ.

The promises of God are only conditional upon one thing – man believing God and entering the promise by faith. And once man entered the promise, his abilities and failures became irrelevant. When God gave Abraham the promise and extended the promise to his descendants, when Abraham failed, the promise did not fail. When Abraham's sons failed, the promise remained sure – because the promise was based upon God's character – not man's.

Each time man was given something by promise, God was the guarantee – not those receiving the promise. We are given the promise of righteousness and eternal life through Christ. He is the guarantee, and we enter that promise by faith. Then nothing annuls God's word, for He is the guarantee, not you. This is the guarantee of your promise, **Romans 4:4-5**

> [4] Now to him who works, the wages are not counted as grace but as debt.
>
> [5] But to him who does not work but believes on Him who justifies the ungodly, his faith is accounted for righteousness,

---

[74] James 2:10, Deuteronomy 11:26-28

If you continue reading the next few verses, the Bible promises that those under this promise are triple-blessed. They are blessed because their sins are forgiven. They are blessed because they are declared as being righteous, apart from their own works. They are blessed because the Lord will not impute (or credit) them with any future sin.

The one who uses religion or personal effort to obtain righteousness is never accounted as righteous. The above passage says that any work we try to do for God by our own efforts is not accounted as righteousness, but as our debt – which is our debt to sin. But the one who does not work, but trusts in the completed work of God promised through Christ, this person is justified and credited as being righteous.

Justified means to be measured against the law and be declared as completely just, and not having any guilt that would require the penalty of the law. And the promise is that God accounts those who are ungodly as justified through Christ.

He was accounted as guilty for your sins, and you are accounted as righteous and just because of His righteousness. And all God requires of you is faith – to put your trust in what Christ as done for you, and to believe that you are righteous through Christ. You are not righteous for Christ; you are righteous through faith in Christ.

Ephesians 1:6 says that you are accepted by God because you are in the Beloved (who is Christ), and this is for the glory of God's grace. God is glorified when you believe and receive His love for you. Grace is God's favor, given to you for no other reason than the truth that He is love, and He desires to express His love to you.

When you believe in God's gift of righteousness, God is pleased with you. If you try to make yourself righteous, God is not pleased. What's more is that as you learn to live in the gift of righteousness through the new spirit you are given, your behavior will begin to align with God's character.

Those who are born again, which are those who receive the gift of righteousness and the gift of a new spirit, whose life is Christ, are saved and pleasing to God.

This is why the Bible says that it is the goodness of God that leads us to repentance. Those who get a glimpse of the new life God has provided are the ones who gladly turn from their sinful old life and toward the new life grounded in God's righteousness. And this is what repentance means. It means to turn from something to another. It is the mind that changes its focus from the world to the abundant life of the Spirit.

There is nothing complicated about accepting Christ. After explaining that the law makes us guilty, the Bible then explains that believing and confessing Christ through faith gives us new life. Look at **Romans 10:9-11**

> [9] that if you confess with your mouth the Lord Jesus and believe in your heart that God has raised Him from the dead, you will be saved.
>
> [10] For with the heart one believes unto righteousness, and with the mouth confession is made unto salvation.
>
> [11] For the Scripture says, "Whoever believes on Him will not be put to shame."

Ephesians 2:8-9 tells you that you are saved by grace through faith. It is a gift of God, not of works. No one can boast, because our works mean nothing to God, but all God's works are given to us.

Look at the promise of life and righteousness. Jesus carried your sins to the cross and was put to death for you. He was raised from the grave in new life as proof that He has the power to give you new life in Himself. God now invites you to put your trust in His works, and then confess your trust in Christ. Then you have the absolute assurance that you can never again be brought into shame. This is what it means to be saved.

If you have never been born again, God's invitation stands. Many have 'committed' their lives to Christ, but this isn't salvation.

Salvation is not what you give to God, but receiving what He has given to you.

The words you say are not magical. The prayer doesn't have to be said in just the right way or with the right words. All that matters is that you are trusting in Christ by receiving His gift of life to you. Speak to God through prayer, giving Him your sins in exchange for His righteousness through Christ. Here is a sample prayer that can guide you if you need it.

Lord, I believe in your promise of life. I believe your promise to forgive all my sins and cleanse me from all unrighteousness. I give you my old life. I trust you with the only thing I have to give – my sins. I'm giving you my sins. I'm giving you my trust. I believe you raised me with Christ, and I receive the promise that You have given me Your righteousness. I believe you have raised me into a new spirit. I believe all things have passed away and now You have made all things new. I confess Jesus as my Lord and Savior. Thank you for the gift of Salvation. Thank you for my new life in Christ. Amen.

As a declaration of starting a new life in Christ, the Bible commands us to be baptized. Baptism is the outward representation of what has happened in your life. The water represents the Spirit who puts your old life into the grave, and when you emerge, that represents a new resurrected life through the power of God. It is the launching of a new life in Christ, where old things have passed away, and all things have become new.

Therefore, I encourage you to find a place where you can be baptized, and begin this new amazing walk of the life of the Spirit!

Other Recent Books by Eddie Snipes

The Revelation of Grace. The first book in the Founded Upon Grace Series. Discover the biblical truths that explain the defeat of sin, and the unveiling of our position in Christ!

Learn to rest in the finished work of Christ! This book provides a solid overview of the Christian life, what it means to walk by faith, and how to live in the Spirit. This book also dispels many misconceptions that the church believes by focusing on the certainty of what we have by promise.

Most Christians spend their life trying to make their flesh act like a Christian, however, the Bible says that the flesh is dead because of sin, but our spirit is life because of God's righteousness. God has declared that it's His job to subdue your sins. Your role is to learn to walk in the Spirit of Grace!

More books from this author:
- The Victorious Christian Life: Living in Grace and Walking in the Spirit.
- The Promise of a Sound Mind : God's plan for emotional and mental health
- Abounding Grace: Dispelling Myths and Clarifying the Biblical Message of God's Overflowing Grace
- Living in the Spirit: God's Plan for you to Thrive in the Abundant Life

www.ingramcontent.com/pod-product-compliance
Lightning Source LLC
Chambersburg PA
CBHW060948050426
42337CB00052B/2582